Bible
StoryBoards

YOU CAN KNOW AND SHARE THE STORY
OF THE BIBLE WITH 15 SIMPLE PICTURES

David and Bernice Gudgel

1218

BIBLE STORYBOARDS
Copyright © 2015 David & Bernice Gudgel
Artwork by Andy Bates
Printed by CreateSpace
www.createspace.com

Library of Congress Cataloging-in-Publication Data
Gudgel, David R. and Bernice Gudgel
Bible StoryBoards / David R. Gudgel, and Bernice Gudgel.
Includes bibliographical references.

ISBN-13: 978-1500450670
ISBN-10:1500450677

Contents

INTRODUCTION

Though the Bible is the bestselling book of all time, the vast majority of people have no idea what it's really all about. That was my story for many years.

My parents gave me my first Bible when I graduated from elementary school, but I wasn't much of a reader so it simply sat on a shelf in my bedroom. As far as I knew it was just another book and I didn't really read books unless I had to for school. So for a long time I had no idea how valuable that Bible could be to me if I would just get to know it.

Later in my teen years I actually started to read the Bible and it began to change my life. The more I read, the more I realized that the Bible wasn't just a bunch of random stories I had heard in Sunday School as I was growing up – stories about Adam & Eve, and a giant flood, and a burning bush, and Samson, and a baby born in a stable. But those were all just part of one grand story that God wanted me to hear and understand.

I eventually became a pastor and committed my life to helping people understand the Bible. And over the years I've realized that my initial experience with the Bible was not that unusual. The vast majority of people who own Bibles just leave them sitting on a shelf. And when they do attempt to check it out, the overall story of the Bible often gets lost in the midst of the familiar stories that they've heard before.

That's why, after teaching hundreds of Bible seminars around the world and preaching thousands of sermons, in Bible StoryBoards we use fifteen simple but memorable pictures to explain the story of God's unfailing desire to have a relationship with us. That's the message of the Bible and it's honestly the greatest love story ever told.

That's right. The Bible is a love story. It tells of God's love for us and His relentless pursuit of a relationship with us. Think about that for a minute. The God of the universe, the maker of heaven and earth, wants to have a personal relationship with each one of us. That may be hard to believe, but it's true.

But, as with any great story, there's a problem that has to be overcome before you get to the happy ending. And in God's love story the problem is us. As God has relentlessly pursued us, we have played hard to get. We've turned away. We've used Him for our benefit and then gone our own way. Over and over again.

In this book we will walk you through the simple story of God that is found in the Bible and His pursuit of a relationship with people like you and me. We will show you the progress of that story through fifteen key periods of history that are described in the Bible.

For each of our fifteen Bible Storyboards you will find the following information:

- Storyboard picture
- Title
- Simple storyline for that era
- Chart
- Expanded storyline for those who want to dig deeper and find out more
- Some things for you to think about
- An opportunity for you to draw the storyboard picture yourself

It is our hope that Bible StoryBoards will help you tap into the life-changing potential that is found in God's Word, that you will be forever changed by what you learn, and that you will then share this amazing story with others.

StoryBoard 1

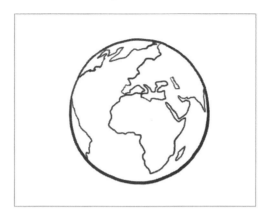

Beginnings

In the beginning God created the heavens and earth. It was the beginning of everything we know and everything we are. That story is told in the first two chapters of Genesis, the book aptly named for its focus on the beginning of the world.

Though our brains can't understand how it happened, God took a barren planet and turned it into the world that we now know. Continents, oceans, jungles, mountains & valleys, fruit trees, wildflowers... Birds, wolves, elephants, dolphins... and man, beginning with Adam & Eve. He created it all for one purpose – so people could walk with Him, and with each other, in a loving relationship.

Beginnings

BIG IDEA	God creates a perfect world to share with mankind.
Bible Book	Genesis 1-2
Main Cast	God Adam & Eve
# of Years	Infinite Past
Key Verse	*Genesis 1:1 - In the beginning God created the heavens and the earth.*

Dig Deeper Into the Storyline

The Bible opens with this amazing and humanly incomprehensible claim: *In the beginning God created the heavens and the earth* (Genesis 1:1). We are told that the planet was covered with water and darkness, and the Spirit of God moved over the waters and spoke the world as we know it into existence.

- It began with light. Then darkness and light were separated and they became day and night. That was Day One.
- Then God created the atmosphere that surrounds earth. The waters below were separated from the waters above in the sky. Day Two.
- On Day Three God caused the water to be separated by dry land. Then He covered the

land with plants of all kinds, bearing seeds and fruit.

- Then God set the planets in motion around the sun so the earth would have days and seasons and years. The sun would govern the day and the moon would govern the night. And the stars began twinkling up through the night sky. That was Day Four.
- Living creatures were then placed in the seas and the skies. Day Five.
- Day Six was a busy day. God created all the animals and creeping things that live on the land. Cattle and snakes and squirrels… And then God made man. Unique out of all the other created things, human beings were made in the image of God. First Adam and then Eve.

God looked at all He had created and saw that it was good. He placed Adam and Eve in a part of the world (somewhere in what we call the Middle East today) that was called the Garden of Eden. He blessed them and told them to rule over the world and to have children and fill the world with people. People who would walk in a loving relationship with God and each other.

Think It Over

The information the Bible gives us about how God created the world is mind-boggling for us humble humans. We can't really wrap our heads around it. How did He do it? How is it possible that a whole lot of something was created out of nothing? Did it all happen in six literal days? Or was it actually six eras of time? And where did God come from anyway? So many questions.

Some things in life, this side of heaven, will go unanswered. But we can be sure of this: the Bible from beginning to end goes to great lengths to answer the *why* question. *Why* did God make the heavens and the earth? The sun and the moon? Trees and animals? Oceans and fish? Men and women and families and food and…well… everything? *Why?*

The *why* is what Bible StoryBoards is all about. It's the bottom line of the story God tells from the first to the last page of the Bible. And the answer is simple: God created the world and people because He wants to have a genuine loving relationship with us, and He wants us to have a genuine loving relationship with each other, forever.

God and a relationship with Him were at the center of everything for the first two humans. It was only natural for them to walk and talk with Him. To honor Him. To acknowledge how great and awesome He was. To want to please the one who had given them life and a perfect world to live in.

In the Garden of Eden, life was like God intended it to be. Perfect and complete. No pain. No fear. No sickness. God and man living life together in perfect harmony. Wouldn't it be great if life could be like that again?

Where everyone enjoyed a perfect loving relationship with God and with each other?

Nothing would please God more. It's what He's wanted from the beginning of time. It's why He created this world. And for a while God had that kind of relationship with Adam & Eve. We're not told how long that lasted, but we do know this - God still longs to have that kind of relationship with man. Forever. The depth of that longing will be seen in the Bible StoryBoards that follow, as we see the astonishing story of what God did, and continues to do, to bring us into a loving relationship with Him, forever.

You'd think mankind would jump at the opportunity to live in vital communion with the God of the universe. Well... think again. And so the story continues...

Try Drawing It Yourself

Use the following simple sketch as an example and try drawing StoryBoard 1 to illustrate *Beginnings*.

StoryBoard 2

Sin

Adam & Eve were placed in a perfect world so together they could enjoy a relationship with God. There was only one thing God told them not to do. He told them not to eat from one particular fruit tree that was in the Garden of Eden. And what did Adam & Eve do? They did that one thing. They ate the fruit from that one forbidden tree. And with that one bad decision, sin entered the world and everything changed. They were driven out of the Garden of Eden and life became very hard. Yet God continued to provide for them and care for them.

As the population of the world grew, sin also spread among mankind. Things eventually got so bad that God sent a flood to wipe out all those who refused to turn from their wickedness and turn back to God. Yet God provided a way of escape through **Noah** and his family.

After the flood, the world began repopulating through Noah's descendants. For a time mankind walked with God again, but eventually they chose to turn from God and to their own sinful ways once again. But this time, instead of sending another flood and starting over again, God miraculously caused the people to begin speaking in different languages at the **Tower of Babel.** As the people grouped together with those they could understand, they ended up spreading throughout the known world. God's desire was that in these smaller groups they would remember their need for Him and turn back to Him.

Sin

BIG IDEA	Man messes up and paradise is lost.
Bible Book	Genesis 3-11
Main Cast	Adam & Eve Noah
# of Years	2000+ years
Key Verse	*Genesis 2:17 - "But you must not eat from the tree of the knowledge of good and evil, for when you eat of it you will surely die."*

Dig Deeper Into the Storyline

The next time you think about doing something God's said not to do, you may want to bring to mind the stories of Adam & Eve, Noah, and the tower of Babel. Remembering what happened in those historical events might keep you from making a really bad decision that could have serious consequences.

God had placed **Adam & Eve** in a gorgeous world that He had created just for them to enjoy with Him and to fill with their descendants. His plan was for the human race to love Him and each other. There was just one thing He asked them not to do. He told them to not eat the fruit of one particular tree. That's it. Just one tree. And He warned them that if they ate that fruit, they would die.

And what did Adam & Eve do? They ate that fruit. And because of that choice, sin entered the world for the first time. The consequences were devastating in their relationship with God, and with each other, and for the world itself. So much was lost because of that one bad decision. Among other things, they lost intimacy with God, a perfect home, marital harmony, painless childbirth, perfect children, sweat-less work, perfect health, and life without death. They went from having it all to struggling to have anything at all, because they chose to put their will above God's.

And it didn't stop there. Sin multiplied as their

descendants multiplied. Murder entered the world. Violence and corruption spread and filled the land. Mankind continued to choose to do things that were evil. Eventually God decided enough was enough. He chose **Noah** to build an ark that would save all those who turned back to God and got on that ark with Noah. Then He sent a flood that destroyed all those who chose to ignore God's message through Noah. Sadly, only Noah, his family, and a select number of animals were spared. When the floodwaters left, God pushed the reset button and started over with Noah and his family. He gave them the charge to repopulate the earth and to call people to once again lovingly live in connection with God and each other.

But once again, as the population grew, man abandoned God's ways in exchange for their own. God had told Noah and his descendants to spread throughout the earth. Instead, mankind settled in one place and began building a city with a very tall tower that would reach up into the heavens. Here they planned to make a name for themselves that they believed would be even above God's name. They didn't think they needed God because they were such a strong and mighty people. God, however, put an end to their plans by miraculously causing various groups of them to speak in different languages. There was no longer one common language for all of mankind. The natural result was for people to gather with those they could understand and move out into the world to claim different areas where each language group would live. This was the beginning of the world as we know it. That tower later became known as the **Tower of Babel** and it was a constant reminder of how foolish it is to turn away from God and a loving relationship with Him.

Think It Over

In spite of God's best efforts to encourage mankind to walk with Him in love, from the very beginning humans have continued to choose to do what was right in their own eyes instead of following God's ways. And we do the same thing today. Sin is now a part of our very nature.

Yet God's relentless pursuit of a loving relationship with people like us is evident from the moment sin came into the world. Immediately following Adam and Eve's sin, God promised to send someone who would defeat Satan and his work in the world (Gen 3:15). Then God graciously provided clothing for His disobedient children and removed them from the Garden of Eden so they wouldn't be able to continue eating from the tree of life, which would have caused them to live forever in their sin, separated from God. Why bother? Because God longed to be in a loving relationship with man.

Later, in Noah's time, God patiently put off the flood for 120 years (Gen 6:3) in the hopes that man would turn from his sinful ways and return to God. And even at the end, when He was ready to wipe out the earth and start over with Noah and his family, God offered His forgiveness and life to any who would come back to Him and get on the boat with Noah. But no one came.

God's incredible love is also evident at Babel when man's sin and pride turned them away from God again. And though God could have chosen to wipe mankind out again, He didn't. He chose instead to tenderly and cleverly scatter them throughout the world so that they might have another opportunity to walk in a loving relationship with Him and each other.

More than a thousand years after these events, God spoke again of His longing for a relationship with people like us. He said, "I have loved you with an everlasting love; I have drawn you with loving-kindness." (Jer. 31:3) That is certainly evident from His interaction with Adam & Eve, Noah, and the people of Babel.

Try Drawing It Yourself

Use the following simple sketch as an example and try drawing StoryBoard 2 to illustrate *Sin*.

StoryBoard 3

Chosen People

As the population of the world grew once again, God knew from experience that simply asking people to continue in a loving relationship with Him and each other was not going to work. We humans kept messing it up. So God's plan for saving men from their own sinfulness was put into motion.

Out of the entire world, God chose Abraham. Though Abraham was far from perfect, God promised to work through him and his descendants to provide a way of salvation for all mankind. Through four generations Abraham's family continued to grow and God's promise was passed down: from Abraham to Isaac; from Isaac to Jacob; from Jacob to his twelve sons. Then through an incredible adventure filled with favoritism, jealousy, treachery, dreams, suffering, and unexpected good fortune, God used Joseph, a descendant of Abraham, to bring the family out of famine in their homeland and into prosperity in Egypt.

God decided to connect with the world by choosing one man and his descendants. He set this family apart in a special way and promised that through them the entire world could be drawn back into a right relationship with Him. What man couldn't do on his own, God would do. God proved once again that His faithfulness and love aren't dependent on ours. God does what He promises, in spite of our failures and shortcomings. That is clearly seen in the people God chose to bless the world through. Perfectly imperfect people like Abraham, Isaac, Jacob, and Joseph.

Chosen People

BIG IDEA	God launches His plan to bring imperfect people back into a relationship with Him.
Bible Books	Genesis 12 – Exodus 2
Main Cast	Abraham, Isaac, Jacob, Joseph
# of Years	645 years
Key Verse	*Genesis 12:2a, 3b - "I will make you into a great nation and I will bless you…and all peoples on earth will be blessed through you."*

Dig Deeper Into the Storyline

God looked down on all the people of the world, who were now spread throughout the known world based on the languages they spoke, and He chose Abram. Abram wasn't perfect. He was simply an ordinary man who had a heart for God. But through Abram God promised to bless the entire world. And through his descendants God promised to provide the way for man to once again walk with God in the loving relationship He had desired from the beginning. What man could not do on his own, God was going to do for them.

God gave Abram a new name – **Abraham**. But for Abraham to live up to his new name, God had to do what Abram could not. You see, Abraham means "father of a multitude." But for the first half of Abram's life nothing was farther from the truth. Abram had no children. There were no descendants on his family tree. Yet God had promised to bless the world through his descendants. So his new name became the reminder of that promise. And what God promises, He delivers: a new home in a new land; the birth of a great nation; public acclaim; an heir that would impact the entire world. All of that would eventually come. But first God led Abram and his wife Sarai to Canaan where they established a new home. They prospered and accumulated property and animals and servants. And finally, when Abraham was one hundred years old and Sarah was ninety (and past childbearing!) God miraculously gave them a son.

They named their son Isaac (which means laughter) because Sarai had laughed when God told them she was going to get pregnant and have a son. Isaac was born fourteen years after Ishmael, the son Abraham had with a servant because Sarai was impatient with God. Abraham's name (father of a multitude) had become a joke since he continued to have no children. So Abraham and Sarai tried to bring God's promise about on their own terms. They decided Abraham's son could be born through a servant. Their impatience led to a slew of problems in and outside their home. Even today, the Arabs, Ishmael's descendants, are still in conflict with the Jews. When Isaac, the true son that God had promised, was finally born fourteen years later, God demonstrated yet again that He does what He says, even when we mess things up.

Isaac, not Ishmael, was then given the promise that God had made to Abram. He was now the chosen one whose descendants God would bless the world through. Isaac grew up and married Rebekah, but they remained childless for twenty years. Finally, after years of prayers, in God's perfect timing Rebekah gave birth to twin sons, Esau and Jacob. Although Esau was the first one born, Jacob was given the birthright privilege and the promise of God. Through his descendants the world would be blessed. Man's ways are not necessarily God's ways.

Jacob and his wife, Rachel, have one of the most

interesting relationship stories in the Bible. He fell in love with Rachel, but was tricked into marrying her older sister, Leah, before their father would let him marry Rachel. So Jacob ended up married to both Rachel and Leah. Not an ideal situation. And it gets even weirder. Through Leah, Rachel, and their two maids, Jacob (whose name God changed to Israel) fathered twelve sons and one daughter. These twelve sons were known as the children of Israel, and many years later their descendants became the twelve tribes of Israel.

Two of these twelve sons prominently stand out in God's story: Judah was the son who inherited the covenant God had made with Abraham and Isaac and Jacob/Israel. God would one day bless the entire world through one of Judah's descendants. And then there was Joseph. **Joseph** was one of the two sons Jacob had with Rachel, the wife that he truly loved. Joseph was Jacob's favorite, and the other brothers knew it. So some of his brothers secretly sold Joseph into slavery and claimed that he had been killed by a wild animal. As a slave, Joseph was taken down into Egypt where God eventually brought him into a position of power. What his brothers meant for evil, God worked for good. During a time of great famine in Canaan, Joseph's family came to Egypt for help, not knowing that Joseph was alive and well and powerful in that country. Joseph ultimately was used by God to save Jacob and His entire family, as they all moved to Egypt.

Think It Over

Two years after Noah died, Abraham was born, which was about 400 years after the devastating flood. The world's population was still relatively small and the nation of Israel did not exist. When Abraham was seventy-five years old, God chose him out of all the people in the world to become the father of a family through whom the entire world would be blessed.

It's important to remember that although Abraham was a man of great faith, he was far from perfect. On at least two separate occasions Abraham cunningly lied about his relationship with Sarah in order to save his neck. Both times, God intervened to accomplish His plan in spite of Abraham's lack of faith (Gen 12:10-20; 20:1-18). The same was seen when Sarah and Abraham impatiently had a child through Hagar (Gen 16:1-15). Once again God, in His time, fulfilled His promise, in His way, and gave them Isaac in their old age (Gen 21:1-8).

Isaac, the son of promise, grew up and married Rebekah. On one occasion when asked by a group of men if Rebekah was his wife, he lied and said she was his sister, just like his dad had done. And once again God graciously intervened and brought the truth to light and protected his chosen imperfect servant from harm (Gen 26:7-11). Eventually Rebekah gave birth to Esau and Jacob, which led to a split in the home because Isaac favored Esau and Rebekah loved Jacob (Gen 25:28). But God's plan, that the older son would serve the younger son (Gen 25:23), trumped man's plan. The birthright went to Jacob in spite of Isaac's bent toward Esau.

God's willingness to keep His promises in spite of man's attempts to do things their own way is again seen in Jacob, who was far from perfect. Having secured the birthright by deception (Gen 27:1-29), Jacob later got paid back when Rachel's father tricked him into marrying Leah first (Gen 29:21-25). But God's will always prevails. In spite of deception gone wild, God gave Jacob twelve sons whose descendants would eventually become a great nation. And from one of those sons, Judah, would come the Messiah who would change the world and would provide the way for us to have an eternal relationship with God.

Joseph, the favored son of Jacob, was envied by his brothers. That jealousy led to incredible trials for Joseph as he was sold into slavery in Egypt. Though everything seemed to be going against him, God ultimately brought Joseph to a place of prominence and power in Egypt. And in God's perfect timing and plan, He used Joseph to save this chosen family that He had promised to use to bless the world.

The story of God's work in and through man includes both faith and failure on the part of many imperfect people. The good, the bad, and the ugly. Thankfully God's plan to share a personal relationship with us is not dependent on our perfection, but on His mercy and grace. He loves us and continues to seek a relationship with us, in spite of who we are.

Try Drawing It Yourself

Use the following simple sketch as an example and try drawing StoryBoard 3 to illustrate *Chosen People*.

StoryBoard 4

Moses

After Joseph died, the rest of his family was no longer in favor with the Egyptians and they eventually became slaves for the next 400 years. But during that time while the children of Israel were suffering as slaves in Egypt, this family through whom God had promised to bless the world grew to several million people.

God's promise to Abraham of many descendants had come true in a big way. Yet they were two million slaves, trapped in a foreign land. But God had not abandoned them. He reached out and saved the children of Israel. Through many incredible signs and miracles, God used Moses (one of Abraham's descendants) to lead them to freedom. At one point God even parted the waters of the sea so they could escape from the Egyptians who were pursuing them.

During this time Abraham's descendants became a mighty nation of people. God led them to the edge of the homeland He had promised them, and He gave them the Ten Commandments – special instructions about how to live in a loving relationship with Him and with others. These commandments would forever set them apart from the rest of the world so God could bless the world through them.

Moses

BIG IDEA	God rescues and instructs His people.
Bible Books	Exodus 2 – Leviticus
Main Cast	Moses
# of Years	80 years
Key Verse	*Exodus 3:8,10a - "So I have come down to rescue them from the hand of the Egyptians and to bring them up out of that land into a good and spacious land, a land flowing with milk and honey. So now, go. I am sending you."*

Dig Deeper Into the Storyline

Most people are familiar with the story of Moses, partly because of the epic movie *The Ten Commandments*.

During his first forty years Moses lived a very privileged life in Egypt and didn't even realize he was one of the children of Israel, who were slaves and were known as the Hebrews. When he found out who he really was, he ended up murdering an Egyptian who was abusing a Hebrew slave. He then fled to the wilderness where he lived for forty years as a shepherd until God miraculously spoke to him from a burning bush. God wanted Moses to go set the two million children of Abraham and Isaac and Jacob free from slavery in Egypt and to lead them back to Canaan, the land He had promised them.

Moses didn't think he was qualified to be a great leader or a deliverer, so he initially rejected God's plan for rescuing the children of Israel from slavery. He told God He had chosen the wrong man and justified his incompetence with five excuses: (1) I'm not qualified, (2) I wouldn't know what to say, (3) The Egyptians won't listen to me, (4) I'm terrible at public speaking, and (5) I just can't do this. But God knew what He was doing and He had a perfect solution for every excuse Moses came up with. First and most importantly, God promised He would go with Moses and give him whatever he needed, including a powerful staff through which miracles would be done and a spokesperson, his brother Aaron, who would handle the public speaking for Moses.

Moses eventually signed on and did what God asked him to do. His work began with facing the Egyptian

Pharaoh and demanding in the name of the Lord that he let God's chosen people go. As God expected, Pharaoh said NO! and then made life even harder on the children of Israel. God then sent a series of ten plagues which not only showed that the God of Israel was greater than the gods the Egyptians worshipped, but they also made the Egyptians miserable! Frogs and locust and sores and water turning to blood... not good. Yet even after nine horrible plagues, Pharaoh still refused to free God's people from slavery.

God then sent one final plague that would kill every first-born child in the land. Yet He offered a way of escape for the children of Israel. All those who took the blood of a lamb and painted it on the front doorpost of their home were spared. God told death to simply *pass over* their houses. But for the Egyptians and those who didn't follow God's instructions, it was a night of death. With every Egyptian home, including Pharaoh's, grieving the loss of their first-born, Pharaoh finally gave in. He called for Aaron and Moses to take the children of Israel and their herds and their flocks and go.

The book of Exodus gets its name from the massive exodus of God's people from Egypt. Picture in your mind the runners who are all squished together behind the starting line at the beginning of a marathon. With 2.5 to 3.5 million fleeing out of Egypt before Pharaoh could change his mind again, the line was really really long. Some mathematicians calculate that if the people were lined up forty in a row, it would have taken sixteen hours for those at the end of the line to get out of town.

The journey from Egypt back to the land of Canaan was roughly 250 miles. God Himself led them with a cloud during the day and a pillar of fire at night. All they had to do was follow. But less than a week into their journey the children of Israel found themselves boxed in by mountains to the north and south, the Red Sea in front of them, and the Egyptian army coming after them from behind. Pharaoh once again had changed his mind.

One can only imagine the overwhelming fear the people at the back of the line felt when they saw the Egyptian chariots chasing them. The people began complaining, yet Moses chose to trust God and he told the people to take their stand and watch God save them. God continued leading the people toward the Red Sea and when Moses reached the shore he stretched out his hand over the water and God miraculously rolled the waters back. God's people then ran across the sea on dry land between two walls of water. Once they were all on the other side, the water fell back into place again and the Egyptians were drowned. The children of Israel were free.

Their journey back to Canaan included many miraculous events as God provided for them in the desert. He gave them bread (called Manna) to gather in the morning, and quail to eat at night, and clean water. They followed the cloud/fire when it moved, and stopped when it stopped. At one point they camped near Mt

Sinai for a year. It was there that God called Moses up onto the mountain alone and gave him the Ten Commandments along with other instructions for the children of Israel. All of these instructions focused on two key priorities: loving God and loving each other. There were also detailed instructions on how to build a transportable worship center (called a Tabernacle) where God could meet with man. God's most important request of His chosen people was that they continue to lovingly follow Him and His ways, and that they not turn away and worship other gods.

Moses was up on the mountain with God for forty days. With all that God had done to deliver the children of Israel from slavery in Egypt – and in doing so, keep the promises He had made to Abraham, Isaac, and Jacob – along with the miracles He had performed already in the desert, you'd think His chosen people could have held out for forty days waiting for Moses to come back with God's further instructions. Well...think again.

When Moses came down from the mountain with the Ten Commandments, he found the people had decided that God and Moses had abandoned them, so they started doing things their own way. They even made a new god out of gold. Since the Egyptians worshiped cows (among many other things), they built a golden calf and called it their new god. They also appointed Aaron to lead them onward. Neither God nor Moses were happy when they saw what the people were doing. Moses angrily threw down the tablets that God had written the Ten Commandments on, shattering them into pieces. Then he cried out to God on behalf of the people and begged for His mercy.

In spite of their sin, God once again gave the people another chance to turn back to Him. Those who did were saved. Those who didn't died. God then made a new set of tablets and the people once again began to follow Him and His commands as they moved through the desert to the homeland He had promised them.

I'm guessing that Moses was clueless about all that would be ahead of him when God called to him out of that burning bush and told him to lead the children of Israel out of Egypt and back to the land of promise. Yet God knew, and He used Moses to accomplish His work through that incredible adventure.

Think It Over

Right in the middle of the journey of God's people from Egypt to the Promised Land, God reached a boiling point and almost gave up on them. After the incident with the golden calf, the Lord said to Moses:

"I have seen these people and they are a stiff-necked people. Now leave me alone so that my anger may burn against them and that I may destroy them. Then I will make you into a great nation."
Exodus 32:9-10

Enough was enough. God was ready to start over again

with Moses, like He had done before with Noah and with Abraham, in His unrelenting desire to have a loving relationship with man. Human beings just kept messing up, no matter what God did to connect with them.

Ever since they had gotten the okay from Pharaoh to leave Egypt, it had been one thing after another with the children of Israel. Pretty much from day one they moaned and complained about everything: *Moses wasn't qualified to be a leader; they had been brought to the edge of the Red Sea to be trapped by the Egyptians and die; water was poisoned or non-existent; there was no food; their living conditions were terrible in comparison to how good they had it in Egypt; manna, manna, manna – the same food day after day; Moses had gone up onto Mt Sinai with God and probably died and now they were all alone*. Complaint after complaint.

If you take some time to read the Exodus account, you'll be hard pressed to find words of gratitude, thanksgiving, or praise of any kind from the people toward God or Moses. Even though they were seeing God's love and grace and patience demonstrated day after day in miraculous ways! A cloud or pillar of fire moving in front of them to show them the way to go? Escaping from the Egyptians by a miraculous walk through the Red Sea? Fresh cold water pouring out of a rock in the middle of a dry desert? Waking up each morning to fresh bread simply lying on the ground outside their tents? Quail just standing there waiting for them to grab and cook for dinner? Seriously? They saw all of this and yet continued to complain and turn away from God. In fact, during this journey they severely tested God's patience seven times.

After seven times of nonsense, when it came to the golden calf God was ready to throw in the towel and start over. But Moses intervened on behalf of God's name and God's people and who he knew God to be. And God changed His mind (Ex. 32:14) and renewed His commitment to lead these stubborn, hard-headed people that He had chosen back to the Promised Land. And in the midst of God's unending astonishing commitment Moses said:

"The LORD, the LORD, the compassionate and gracious God, slow to anger, abounding in love and faithfulness, maintaining love to thousands, and forgiving wickedness, rebellion and sin…"
Exodus 34:6b-7a

God chose to give His chosen people another chance. And a choice of their own. Once again they could choose to follow God and His ways. To walk with Him and each other in love. Through this incredible journey that God took his people on, we see once again that our compassionate and gracious God, who abounds in loving-kindness, relentlessly pursues a relationship with us.

Try Drawing It Yourself

Use the following simple sketch as an example and try drawing StoryBoard 4 to illustrate *Moses*.

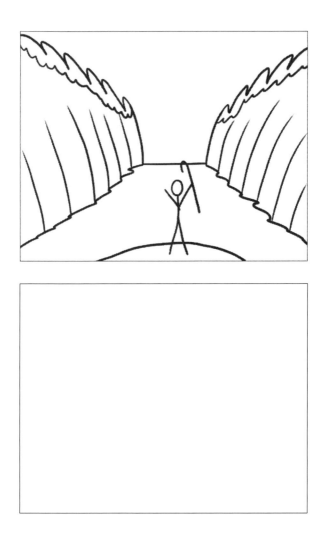

StoryBoard 5

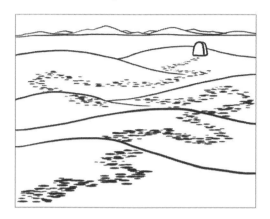

Wandering

The Children of Israel's escape from Egypt and their journey through the desert finally came to an end as they reached the border of Canaan, the land God had promised to Abraham, Isaac, and Jacob. The cloud that God had used to lead them stopped and it was time to take the land for their own.

But even after all they had seen God do during their exodus from Egypt, the people were afraid of the "giants" who were already living in the land. Everyone, except Joshua and Caleb, refused to trust God. Though God told them to go in and take the land, the people thought they knew better and they refused to go in.

So once again they suffered the consequences of turning away from God. The Children of Israel spent the next 40 years wandering aimlessly through the very desert they had just come through. That journey didn't end until every one of the adults who had refused to go in and take the land had died. Once that had happened, Moses repeated God's law to the surviving remnant and reminded them that blessing would come from obeying Him and following Him.

Wandering

BIG IDEA	Fear and unbelief lead to a generation lost.
Bible Books	Numbers – Deuteronomy
Main Cast	Moses, Joshua, Caleb
# of Years	40 years
Key Verse	*Numbers 13:31b - "We can't attack those people; they are stronger than we are."*

Dig Deeper Into the Storyline

After spending almost a year at Mt Sinai, God had **Moses** and the people make final preparations before they began the last 200 miles to the promised land. The children of Israel were divided into twelve tribes, based on whom they had descended from of the sons of Jacob. Then they counted the total number of male descendants in each tribe that were at least twenty years old. Once they got to the promised land, they would need to fight for the land, so they needed to know how many men were capable of going to war. The total number was over 600,000.

One can only imagine the excitement the people must have had when the cloud of the Lord finally lifted and led them away from Mt Sinai toward the end of their journey. In eleven days they would be at the edge of the land God had promised to Abraham, Isaac, and Jacob (Deut. 1:2).

During their journey from Egypt they had seen time and again that God could be trusted to take care of them and to provide for them. They knew from experience that choosing to follow God always turned out to be the best choice. You would think after all they had seen God do for them, they would have been ready to follow God's leading into whatever lay ahead in the promised land.

Finally the day came when the cloud they were following stopped at a place called Kadesh Barnea which was at the edge of Canaan, the land God had promised to them. The tribes of Israel all set up camp and twelve men were selected, one from each tribe, to go into Canaan and secretly spy out the land and then bring back their report so plans could be made for taking over the land. The spies stayed in the land for forty days and thoroughly checked out the entire area, which was 150 miles long and 60 miles wide.

They came back with a very mixed report. On the one hand, they said the land was filled with an abundance of food. They said it was "overflowing with milk and honey!" On the other hand, they said the people were really big and strong, and the cities were also big strong fortresses. And then they added that two tribes of giants also lived in Canaan!

Ten of the spies came to a very unfortunate conclusion. They told the people that if they tried to take the land they would all be slaughtered. The Children of Israel would come to an end. When they heard this news, the people freaked out, wept, grumbled, and decided that they'd be better off appointing a new leader and going back to Egypt.

Caleb and **Joshua**, the other two spies, had a very different opinion. They agreed it was a land flowing with milk and honey. And yes there were strong people and cities there. Even giants! And they agreed that the obstacles ahead of them were insurmountable… humanly speaking. But they also believed God was bigger than the biggest giant or fortress or problem that lie ahead. They passionately pleaded with the people to not give in to fear but to trust God and follow His leading into Canaan. But the people refused to listen to Joshua and Caleb. Once again, they refused to trust God.

This was the tenth time on the journey from Egypt to Canaan that God's people had grumbled, complained, resisted, and turned their back on God's plans and leading. This time God said, "Enough is enough." After all that He had done for them, in Egypt and on their journey, God decided to kill off this entire unbelieving generation. Only Caleb and Joshua and their families, along with those who were nineteen and younger, would be spared. Immediately a plague took the lives of the ten spies who voted against going in to Canaan, and over the next forty years God's unfaithful people wandered around in the desert until that entire unbelieving generation of adults had died in the wilderness.

Once the final death took place, their wandering was over. God gathered the surviving remnant of His people at Moab before giving them another chance to go in and take the promised land that He had sworn to give to the descendants of Abraham, Isaac, and Jacob. Since this new generation was young and many had not even been born when God gave His instructions at Mt Sinai, Moses went over God's commands and instructions and expectations one more time. What was said is revealed in the book of Deuteronomy, the second giving of God's law. Moses gathered God's people and repeatedly called them to love the Lord their God with all their heart and with all their soul and with all their might. In no uncertain terms he reminded them that obedience to the Lord was the path to blessing and that disobedience led to serious consequences.

After spending the past forty years watching their

parents and grandparents die in the wilderness, this new generation was more than ready to hear and obey God's Word through Moses. They didn't want to make the same mistake the previous generation had made. The Children of Israel were now ready to follow the Lord fully, no matter what giants or obstacles lay ahead.

Think It Over

If you pulled out a map and plotted the shortest route from Egypt to Canaan, and then compared it to the way God led the Children of Israel when He first brought them out of Egypt, you'd see He chose the long way home. No doubt the direct route, the coastal route, was much prettier. And for those of us who like to get from point A to point B in the shortest time possible, that route would have made complete sense. But God had another more important agenda in mind.

God chose the long route for two primary reasons. For one, like a protective father, God took his people away from danger.

When Pharaoh let the people go, God did not lead them on the road through the Philistine country, though that was shorter. For God said, "If they face war, they might change their minds and return to Egypt."
Exodus 13:17

If He had led them on the direct route to the promised

land, they would have passed through Philistine country. That was dangerous territory, much like the land of Canaan. But Philistine country was closer to Egypt. If they had faced danger that early in their journey, they could have easily turned and run back to Egypt.

So God chose to lead His people on the longer route, not only to protect them from foolishly running back into slavery, but also to have the time to grow the relationship He had with His chosen people. Everything He did on their journey, as He led them and cared for them and provided for them, was intended to bring them into a closer relationship with Him. He wanted them to learn to trust Him with every part of their being – for their food and water, for their comfort and safety, for their present and future. And most of all He wanted them to learn to know Him. To revere and honor him. To worship Him. To love Him. Year after year on this journey through the desert, God worked in and through the circumstances His people faced to bring them into a deeper relationship with Him.

Throughout the journey their reactions revealed what progress, if any, the people were making in knowing and trusting God.

Remember how the LORD your God led you all the way in the desert these forty years, to humble you and to test you in order to know what was in your

heart, whether or not you would keep his commands.
Deuteronomy 8:2

God was seeking to grow His children up in their love for Him and for others. How did they do? Well I think you'll agree the answer to that question is – not very well. In spite of seeing so many miraculous events happen right before their eyes over and over again, the Children of Israel constantly defaulted to moaning and complaining, ungratefulness, hardheartedness, fear, and flat out disobedience. And it all peaked when they got to the edge of the promised land and the Israelites said "No" to God's command to "Go." Yes there were giants in the land and the challenge before them was huge, but they should have known by then that God was bigger than anyone or anything they would face in Canaan.

Their long-cut home revealed what was in their hearts and eventually killed them. It wasn't supposed to end that way. If they had followed God's commands fully it wouldn't have ended that way. All they had to do was trust God and what they knew to be true of Him, because they had seen it with their own eyes! That's all that God expected of the generation that lost their lives in the wilderness. It's also what He expected of the new generation that heard Moses explain the law once again. It's what God still expects of us today. How we respond to what He expects will reveal the place God truly has in our hearts.

Try Drawing It Yourself

Use the following simple sketch as an example and try drawing StoryBoard 5 to illustrate *Wandering*.

StoryBoard 6

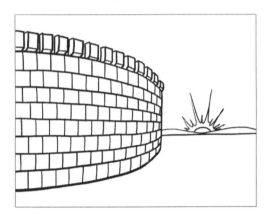

Promised Land

Once again the Children of Israel came to the edge of the homeland God had promised them. And once again God told them to go in and take the land.

Under the faithful leadership of **Joshua**, this time the Children of Israel got it right. Beginning with the walled city of Jericho, they conquered the giants their parents and grandparents had feared. As they continued to do all God commanded, He was with them every step of the way and gave them success. They took over the land of Canaan and made it their own.

Finally, after 440 years away from the land that God had promised to them, they came home and the descendants of Abraham became a mighty nation of people. True to His Word, God made good on His promises.

Promised Land

BIG IDEA	Courage and trust lead to a new homeland.
Bible Book	Joshua
Main Cast	Joshua, Caleb
# of Years	25 years
Key Verse	*Joshua 1:7-9 - "Be strong and very courageous. Be careful to obey all the law my servant Moses gave you... then you will be prosperous and successful..."*

Dig Deeper Into the Storyline

After a string of tragic losses, the children of Israel were about to have a winning streak. Finally. Throughout the previous 400 years as slaves in Egypt and then 40 years of wandering in the desert, God had waited for the day when the children of Abraham, Isaac, and Jacob would trust Him fully, no matter what the odds or obstacles that stood before them. God's chosen people were about to experience the benefit of trusting Him and obeying Him.

The years of wandering finally ended as the last of the unbelieving adults died. The surviving Children of Israel found themselves standing once again at the edge of the land God had promised to give them. Moses and

Joshua and **Caleb** were the only elders who remained alive. Moses explained once again the laws and instructions God had given to them, then he too died without ever entering the Promised Land.

After Moses' death, leadership responsibilities for this family who had become a nation were given to Joshua. God's charge for Joshua was clear. Three times He told him to "be strong and courageous" (Joshua 1:6,7,9). Strength, courage, and unquestioned obedience to everything God commanded were the prerequisites for success. Joshua was not to give in to fear but instead he was to trust God and follow His leading. No matter what. If he and the Children of Israel did that, God promised to give them the land that lay before them as their home. Success and prosperity would be theirs.

Joshua passed this charge and challenge on to his leaders and the people. He made sure they understood that the bottom line was to do whatever God commanded. Then Joshua sent two spies in to check out the land. Unlike the ten spies who had come back with a fear-filled report forty years earlier, these men came back declaring that God was delivering the land into their hands. They believed victory was ahead (Joshua 2:24).

This time the people chose to trust God to give them the victory. They were ready to follow Him in and take the land, so they broke camp and traveled the final seven miles to the Jordan River where they would cross over into the promised land. When they got there, God gave them one final reminder of His power by miraculously parting the waters of the Jordan River and making it possible for the entire nation to cross over on dry land, just as their ancestors had crossed the Red Sea.

The city of Jericho, one of the oldest cities in the ancient world, stood as the first challenge that God's people faced after they crossed the Jordan River. This massive fortified city, protected by walls that were twenty-five feet high and twenty feet thick, was considered invincible by the Canaanites. God told the Children of Israel that it was time to take the city. Though His instructions on how to go about doing that were very unconventional, they chose to be strong and courageous and to trust Him. They obeyed.

One can only imagine what the people of Jericho must have thought when they saw Israel's men of war quietly marching around the city walls, following the ark and seven priests who were each armed with a trumpet. They watched them take one lap around the walls and then peacefully go back to their camp. For six days in a row this seemingly ridiculous ritual was repeated as the residents of Jericho looked on. On the seventh day the same thing happened again, but on that day they circled the city seven times. After the seventh lap, as God had commanded, the seven priests finally blew their trumpets and the men of Israel shouted as loud as they could. Yes, that was God's plan. The priests blew their trumpets. The men yelled. And that's when God's supernatural power took over. The walls of Jericho literally collapsed and the men of Israel ran in and fought to take the city. Their obedience and God's power led them to success. The city was theirs.

For the next seven years, what began at Jericho continued. City after city fell as God's people took the promised land by defeating the people who were living there. Joshua then divided the land among the twelve tribes, and each tribe settled in the area they were given. Success, prosperity, and rest finally came to the descendants of Abraham, Isaac, and Jacob after over four centuries of wandering and waiting. They had become a mighty nation.

Joshua 11:23
So Joshua took the entire land, just as the LORD had directed Moses, and he gave it as an inheritance to Israel according to their tribal divisions. Then the land had rest from war.

Think It Over

Same land. Same circumstances. Same challenge. Same obstacles. Same promise. Same command. Same family. Same God.

Forty years later. Different outcome. Why?

Different time. Different leader. Different people. Different faith. Different choice.

If ever a lesson was learned, this one was. If ever a generation deliberately chose not to be like their parents, this one did. If ever good judgment came after a really bad experience, you see it here. And heaven rejoiced and life-changing victory was the result.

If only their parents and grandparents and great grandparents had had the faith that their children chose to live out, life would have been so much different. So much better. But they didn't. Instead of trusting God, they chose to do what seemed to make sense to them. They thought they knew better, so they turned from God and went their own way... and ended up wandering in the desert until they died.

It's no wonder that God's instructions to Joshua before taking the land can be summarized by the following: "Joshua...be strong and courageous... be strong and courageous...do not fear...do not fear... be strong and courageous....and whatever you do, make sure you do everything I command you... do everything I've commanded you!"

The Children of Israel were finally able to take the land that God had promised them once they chose to trust Him completely. To follow Him without question. Even when what He was asking them to do seemed really weird! But because they chose to obey – because they understood that God was God and they were not – with His help they were able to take first Jericho and then the land as their own.

Several years ago at the Congress On The Bible E.V. Hill was talking about God's Word when he said, "Trust it, don't adjust it." That really is the bottom line, isn't it. Will we trust God's Word? His commands? All of it? An unbelieving generation didn't, and they died in the desert. Joshua did. He was fully surrendered to whatever God wanted. His commitment was:

"As for me and my household, we will serve the LORD."
Joshua 24:15b

Under the leadership of fully surrendered Joshua, God's people gained what God had promised. Fortresses fell. Giants were killed. What was once thought impossible, was possible. Victory was won. God's name was exalted and feared throughout the land. All that and more came from knowing and doing God's Word. Not some of it. All of it. It pays to do everything God says.

Try Drawing It Yourself

Use the following simple sketch as an example and try drawing StoryBoard 6 to illustrate *Promised Land*.

StoryBoard 7

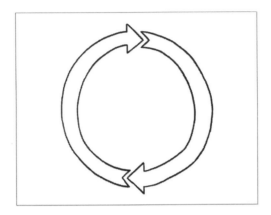

Judges

After their conquest of the promised land, the Children of Israel settled in to their new home. It was a land of great abundance and prosperity. But as life became easy, they forgot how dependent they actually were on God. Instead of following His ways they began doing what was right in their own eyes.

This began a terrible cycle that continued for over 300 years: the people turned away from God – then their peace and prosperity vanished as they were plundered by enemies – then the people turned back to God and cried out for help – then God sent a mighty judge to deliver them from their enemies – then after a time of peace and prosperity, the cycle would begin again as the people turned away from God once again.

The Children of Israel went through this same foolish

cycle many times during the 350 years that are recorded in the book of Judges.

Judges

BIG IDEA	The arrogance of man and the grace of God.
Bible Books	Judges – I Sam 1-8
Main Cast	Deborah, Gideon, Samson, Ruth, Samuel
# of Years	350 years
Key Verse	*Judges 17:6 - In those days Israel had no king; everyone did as he saw fit.*

Dig Deeper Into the Storyline

The era recorded in the book of Judges stands in stark contrast to the time of Joshua. Throughout the days of conquest under Joshua's leadership, the Children of Israel willingly obeyed God. Not so in the time of Judges. The generations that followed Joshua became arrogant in their prosperity and blatantly disobeyed God. They are described as a generation that did not know the Lord or the mighty works He had done throughout their history.

In the midst of their peace and prosperity did they simply forget that they owed it all to God and to His blessing? Did the parents who had seen and experienced God's power at work simply forget to teach their children about it all? Or did sinful human beings simply choose to disregard what they had been told about God and fall back into their own sinful ways? However it happened, the outcome was the same. "Everyone did what was right in his own eyes" (Judges 21:25).

During the 350 years that followed Joshua's death, God's chosen people – the ones He had promised to bless the world through – lived out an *on again/off again* relationship with God. After demonstrating unquestioning faith in God throughout the time of conquest under Joshua's leadership, once they were settled into the land and life became easy, the Children of Israel turned away from the God of their fathers to the gods of their neighbors.

God responded by giving His chosen people over to enemy nations. These other nations and their false gods made the Children of Israel's lives miserable and pulled them into detestable practices. In time, however, the physical and emotional consequences of their bad choices caught up with them. When God's wayward children could take it no longer, they turned back to the Lord under severe distress and cried out for deliverance from their oppressors. Moved by pity, in His love and mercy God sent judges to deliver them from their enemies and they once again were blessed with peace and prosperity. For a while...until once again they forgot about God and turned away from Him again and went back to doing whatever was right in their own eyes. And the cycle would begin again.

Over those years seventeen different judges came to Israel's aid. Thirteen of these deliverers are named in the book of Judges. The remaining four are found in 1 Samuel 1-7. While each judge had a prominent role in delivering God's people from the consequences of their evil ways, four are highlighted in the Old Testament because of their unique stories.

Deborah was a woman who believed God and obeyed Him without hesitation even when others didn't. She led the people to subdue the Canaanite armies.

Gideon initially questioned God's "you're the man" appointment but finally relented and experienced first-hand the power of God. With just 300 men and a bunch of trumpets and pitchers with torches inside, Gideon defeated an army of 135,000 Midianites.

Samson was a man that God had blessed with incredible strength. His potential to do mighty things for God was wasted throughout most of his life because of a woman named Delilah. Yet at the end of his life, God granted his dying request and used his strength to kill more Philistines in his death than during his life.

Samuel was a faithful servant of God who lived out his potential as a judge, a priest, and a prophet.

In spite of the Children of Israel's repeated failure to walk in the ways of the Lord, during the time of the judges not all was bad for God's people. In fact, during those 350 years they lived more years in the Lord's favor than outside of it. God blessed His repentant children with twice as many years of peace than the years of hardship that came their way whenever they turned away from Him.

Another prominent person during this time was **Ruth**. She was not a judge, but she lived during the time of the judges. She wasn't one of the Children of Israel by birth, but she married into the family of God's chosen people. In spite of the disobedience, idolatry, and violence of the time, Ruth clung to the God of Israel and Naomi, her mother-in-law, after her first husband died. Her faithfulness was rewarded when she met a man named Boaz, from the tribe of Judah, whom she eventually married. Ruth became the great-grandmother of David and therefore was an ancestor in the line of the Messiah, the descendant of Abraham, Isaac, and Jacob that God had promised to send to provide the way for mankind to come back into a permanent relationship with Him.

Think It Over

The message of Judges is as relevant today as it was in the days of the judges – perhaps even more so – because now we have the benefit of both hindsight and foresight.

Hindsight gives us the opportunity to look back and learn from our mistakes and the mistakes of others. To look over our shoulder and see what went wrong. To learn from it and hopefully choose to not make the same stupid mistakes again. For the average Joseph living in Canaan during the time of the judges, that would have meant simply asking himself, "Is it really a good idea for me to do what's right in my own eyes? I mean after all the pain that keeps coming our way every time we've done that, maybe it would be better in the future to do what God says is right, rather than what we think is right?"

Over and over the Children of Israel put God to the test by doing things their own way instead of God's way. And over and over we see how God let them suffer the consequences of their foolish choices until they turned back to Him. The wise ones looked back and learned a valuable lesson. "Whatever a person sows, that's what they'll reap." Solomon spoke about that obvious lesson when he said:

> *The wicked man earns deceptive wages, but he who sows righteousness reaps a sure reward.*
> (Proverbs 11:18)

You reap what you sow. You get paid in kind. More than 1000 years later the Apostle Paul wrote similar words:

Do not be deceived, God is not mocked;
whatever a man sows, this he will also reap.
(Galatians 6:7)

Seeing what happened to the Children of Israel during the time of the judges can give us a foresight advantage now. We don't have to make the same mistakes. We can learn from this painful era in their history and accept the fact that doing what we think is right, instead of what God says is right, isn't the path to blessing. It's the path to pain. And we don't have to go that way. We can accept the blessings that God longs to pour out on us if we will simply trust Him and follow Him. But He can't do that if we substitute our way for His.

Now's the time to commit that lesson to memory and be changed by it. Knowing what's right and doing what's right in the eyes of the Lord is the best way to live.

Try Drawing It Yourself

Use the following simple sketch as an example and try drawing StoryBoard 7 to illustrate *Judges*.

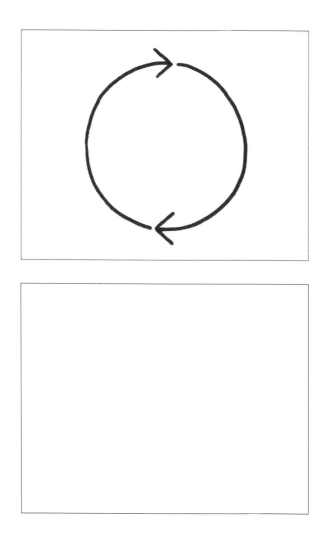

StoryBoard 8

Kings

The time of the judges came to an end when the Children of Israel decided they wanted to be like the nations around them. Having an invisible God leading them was no longer enough. They wanted a human king like everyone else. So they went to Samuel, the judge at that time, and told him to tell God that they wanted a king of their own. Though he reminded them that following God was infinitely better than following any human king, the people wouldn't change their minds. They wanted a king and they wanted him now. So God gave them what they said they wanted. As the era of kings began, the days of the judges came to an end.

Saul was appointed by God as the first king of the nation of Israel. The crown eventually passed to **David** and then his son **Solomon**. This significant change from a theocracy (following God alone) to a monarchy (following a king) led to a whole new era in the history of the descendants of Abraham, Isaac, and Jacob.

Of the thirty-nine kings that followed Saul and David and Solomon, only eight walked with God and followed His leading. The other thirty-one led the Israelites away from God and into sin. Once again, many years and many lives were wasted as the people chose to do what was right in their own eyes instead of following God's ways. Yet throughout these years, God continued to reach out to His chosen people through prophets, beginning with Samuel, whom He sent to warn them about the consequences of their sin and to remind them of His power and love and grace.

Kings

BIG IDEA	God gives men what they think they want.
Bible Books	I Sam 1-8—2 Chronicles Psalms—Song of Sol, Isaiah—Lam, Hos—Zeph
Main Cast	Saul, David, Solomon
# of Years	440 years
Key Verse	*1 Samuel 8:19b-20 - "We want a king over us. Then we will be like all the other nations, with a king to lead us…"*

Dig Deeper Into the Storyline

From the day he was born, Samuel was destined for greatness in the eyes of God, but not necessarily in the eyes of the people. As the last judge and the first prophet, he proved himself capable and faithful. Under his leadership as a judge Israel experienced God's favor even to the extent that God delivered them from the formidable Philistine army. But even after all God did through Samuel's leadership, when it came to heeding Samuel's "you really don't want a king" warnings, the Children of Israel would not be deterred. They wanted a king like all the other nations around them. So God gave in to their demand and gave them **Saul**, the first in a long line of kings that reigned for the next 440 years. The Children of Israel became the kingdom of Israel.

King Saul got this newly established kingdom off to a terrible start. At first, when the Spirit of God was upon Saul, it looked like he was in for a great run. But that all changed when not long into his reign he foolishly ignored God's commands and disobeyed Him. From that point on, for the most part King Saul ignored God and did whatever he wanted to do instead. God eventually regretted that He had made Saul king over Israel and Saul was replaced by **David**, a young shepherd boy who became a mighty soldier and then a king.

David first made a name for himself when as a young man he courageously took on the Philistine giant,

Goliath, whom everyone else was afraid to meet in battle. With only a slingshot and a stone, David killed Goliath and from that point on the son of Jesse, descendant of Judah, was destined for greatness. Because David had a heart for God, the Lord placed His Spirit upon him and caused him to prosper in whatever he did, while Saul's value in the eyes of the people descended because God's Spirit had left him. Saul came to hate David and tried to kill him several times, but God protected David and eventually gave him the privilege of ruling over His people as King for forty years.

The Bible tells us that David had a whole heart for God, but in his humanness his reign as king had its ups and downs. He wrote most of the Psalms, which reflect the ebb and flow of his life and give us a candid look at what his walk with God was like. His obedience to the Lord led to national blessing on Israel during his reign – spiritually, economically, and militarily. The kingdom united and expanded and Jerusalem became the center of civil and religious life for the Children of Israel.

David had it all going for him until the day he foolishly committed adultery with Bathsheba and then tried to cover it up by having her husband killed so he could quickly marry her. Although David finally admitted his sin and God forgave him, David's reign as King was never the same after that. His disobedience had devastating consequences on his life, and his family, and the entire nation.

Solomon, the oldest son of David & Bathsheba, inherited the throne from his father and served as Israel's third king. Like his father, he also had a heart for God, and God placed His Spirit within him. At the outset God gave Solomon the unusual opportunity to ask for whatever he wanted – one thing that God would freely give him, no questions asked. Many would have asked for a long life or fame or riches or the death of one's enemies. Not Solomon. He simply asked for discernment – the ability to make wise decisions in his new role as the King of Israel.

Solomon's request pleased God so much that He not only gave him incredible wisdom but also wealth and fame and the promise of a long life if he continued to walk with the Lord. Eventually people from all over the world came to Israel to hear the wisdom of Solomon. Some of the 3,000 sayings he wrote are found in the book of Proverbs. He built a beautiful temple for God in Jerusalem – something his father had planned for and longed to do. Solomon also had a beautiful palace built for himself. Made out of costly stones, it took thirteen years to build.

There's never been another king like Solomon. As his wealth and fame grew, whatever he wanted he got. Which is not necessarily a good thing. Even though he had it all going for him, he messed up big time – even more than his father. Instead of just one woman, Solomon became involved with over 1,000 foreign women who led his heart away from God (Neh. 13:26).

The incredible but sad story of Solomon's life and reign as King of Israel is spoken of in Ecclesiastes, the book of regrets that he wrote toward the end of his life. Though he spent many wasted years in sin, in the end he came to his senses and turned back to God. In looking back as an old man he wisely concluded that the bottom line of life can be summed up in two things: "fear God and keep his commandments" (Ecc 12:13). That's all that really matters.

When King Solomon's reign ended, once again life changed drastically for the Children of Israel. The nation that had been united under Saul and David and Solomon split into two separate kingdoms with two different kings. Solomon's son Rehoboam ruled over the tribes of Judah & Benjamin and formed the kingdom of Judah in the south. Jeroboam, one of Solomon's former military officers, split off and led the ten northern tribes to independence. He became their king and they became known as the kingdom of Israel. The Children of Israel had now divided into two kingdoms.

The second half of the book of 1 Kings and on through 2 Kings tells the tragic story of sin and idolatry that prevailed over the next 250 years. Things got really bad. Thirty-nine kings reigned over Abraham's descendants during this time. Thirty-one of them didn't care about God and led their people to follow the evil ways of the nations around them. Only eight loved God and led the people to follow Him.

Throughout this difficult time God sent prophets to call the people to turn from their sin and back to Him. Elijah, Elisha, Amos, and Hosea were sent to the northern kingdom of Israel. Obadiah, Joel, Isaiah, Micah, Nahum, Zephaniah, Jeremiah, and Habakkuk were sent to the southern kingdom of Judah. But in spite of God's continuing effort to convince His people to turn from their evil ways, His children refused to listen and were destined once again to suffer the consequences of their choices.

The Israelites persisted in all the sins of Jeroboam and did not turn away from them until the LORD removed them from his presence, as he had warned through all his servants the prophets.
2 Kings 17:22-23a

So the LORD said, "I will remove Judah also from my presence as I removed Israel, and I will reject Jerusalem, the city I chose, and this temple, about which I said, 'There shall my Name be.'"
2 Kings 23:27

Think It Over

A good beginning doesn't guarantee a good end. Israel's first three kings – Saul, David, and Solomon – all learned that lesson the hard way. If we're smart, we'll learn from their failures rather than making the same mistakes ourselves.

In Old Testament times, God placed His Spirit in specific

people for specific situations. He gave **Saul** His Spirit when he became King, which meant Saul had more than enough power to live out God's call on his life. He could have become great in God's eyes. He chose instead to live by his own strength. Determined to make a name for himself and filled with jealousy toward David, King Saul was obsessed with eliminating anyone and everyone who got in the way of his own will being done. He ended up losing God's Spirit and his kingdom.

King **David**, also filled with God's Spirit, grew greater and greater in his impact and accomplishments for God until the day his flesh got the best of him. Bathsheba caught his eye and instead of saying no to temptation, he gave in. And if the sin of adultery wasn't bad enough, he spiraled deeper into sin when he took elaborate cover-up steps, which eventually led to murder. Moses' words, "be sure your sins will find you out" (Numbers 32:23), came true. Not only was David found out, he also discovered firsthand how miserable life can get when you're living under guilt and unconfessed sin. Fortunately for David, he eventually got things squared away with God. He owned up to His sin and experienced the blessing of forgiveness. But even then, the consequences of his fleshly lapse haunted him for the rest of his life.

You'd think **Solomon** would have kept on the straight and narrow path after seeing the consequences of Saul and David's stupidity. It seemed like he had learned from their mistakes when his reign got off to a great start with God. King Solomon had wisdom and wealth and a great wife whom he loved (Read Song of Solomon for their love story). What more could he want?

Well... how about a second wife. And then a third. Then a fourth. Until the day he added wife number 700. Seriously! And if that foolishness wasn't enough, he had an additional 300 concubines, women who weren't his wives but who were there simply for him to have sex with. And all of those women turned his heart away from God. Little by little Solomon drifted into a life that was centered on himself instead of God.

Finally, as an old man Solomon realized that all the women and wealth and fame that he had gathered had left him empty inside. None of it could satisfy. And that's when he remembered that God's way was much better than the sinful selfish ways he had given the middle part of his life to.

Saul, David, Solomon. Three really good people. Each with incredible potential. Destined for greatness. But each one of them blew it. Big time. And they lived to regret it. Even though David and Solomon both got it together before their lives ended, their lives would have been so much better, for them and for the people they were responsible for, if they had stayed in a right relationship with God instead of going their own way.

Stories like this from the Bible are more than just a good read. They are accounts of real people living real lives, with all their strengths and weaknesses. And their stories can keep us from making the same mistakes. With God's help, in His strength, we can live a full and complete life. If you're one of God's children, He's placed His Spirit in you to help you do that. If you stay plugged into God, you can have a good start, a good middle, and a good finish. Nothing would please God more.

Try Drawing It Yourself

Use the following simple sketch as an example and try drawing StoryBoard 8 to illustrate *Kings*.

StoryBoard 9

Consequences

For 450 years God had lovingly sent His prophets to plead with the nations of Israel and Judah – His chosen people – to turn away from their sin and return to following His ways. But even after repeated admonitions, pleadings, and clear warnings, the Lord's stubborn children just would not listen.

So God, like a loving parent, finally let them suffer the consequences of their sin – their enemies overpowered both Israel and Judah. The land that God had helped them conquer under Joshua was taken away from them. The peace and prosperity and freedom that they had enjoyed with God's blessing disappeared.

The Children of Israel spent the next seventy years suffering the consequences of their sinful choices. Yet even during this time of pain and suffering, God continued to reach out to them through the prophets, once again offering them hope if they would trust in God and turn back to Him.

Consequences

BIG IDEA	God's people suffer after turning away from Him again.
Bible Books	2 Kings Amos, Hosea, Ezekiel, Daniel
Main Cast	Jeremiah, Ezekiel, Daniel, Amos, Hosea
# of Years	70 years
Key Verse	*2 Chronicles 36:16 - But they mocked God's messengers, despised his words and scoffed at his prophets until the wrath of the Lord was aroused against his people and there was no remedy.*

Dig Deeper Into the Storyline

So far in the story of God's relationship with man we have seen a definite pattern being repeated over and over. God lovingly reaches out to man in His desire to have a relationship with him. Then man messes up and turns away from God. Consequences are suffered. God reaches out to man again with forgiveness and grace.

An interesting historical event is inserted into the Bible during the time of the prophets that helps us understand more about God and man and their parts in this repeating drama. Before we look at the consequences the nations of Israel and Judah suffered because of their sin, it will be helpful to take a look at the story of Jonah.

Jonah was a prophet. A prophet's job was to warn God's people of the consequences of their sin and to plead with them to turn back to God. But unlike the other prophets, God didn't send Jonah to the Children of Israel. Instead He sent him to one of their enemies, the people of Nineveh. If you remember back to the promise God gave to Abraham, Isaac, and Jacob, He promised to bless the entire world through their descendants. Not just the Children of Israel. So in the midst of His dealings with the stubborn children of Abraham, God chose to reach out to others too.

When God told Jonah that He wanted him to go preach to the people of Nineveh, Jonah refused. The people of Nineveh were a wicked people. They were enemies! And Jonah knew that God was "gracious and compassionate... slow to anger and abundant in loving kindness..." (Jonah 4:2). Jonah didn't want Israel's enemies to turn to God and be forgiven. He wanted them punished! So Jonah tried to run away and hide from God.

But God is God. He used a really big fish to convince Jonah to go and prophesy in the great city of Nineveh. So Jonah went and told the people of Nineveh that they had forty days to "turn from their wicked ways" or else

God would destroy their city. The people heard God's warning, turned from their wicked ways, and turned to God. And as Jonah expected, "God relented concerning the calamity which He had declared He would bring upon them. And He did not do it" (Jonah 3:10). This event reminds us that God longs for everyone everywhere to turn from their sin and come into a relationship with Him.

That's why the Lord sent prophet after prophet to the nations of Israel and Judah during the time of the kings. He wanted His people to repent and turn from their sin and come back to following Him. If they had responded to the message of the prophets like the Ninevites did, God would have forgiven them and they would have avoided the consequences the prophets had warned them of, just like the people living in Nineveh. But the Children of Israel refused to listen to the prophets, so the time of consequences began.

Of the two kingdoms, God judged Israel first. After more than 200 years of disobedience to God's law, nineteen bad kings, and the Israelites' unwillingness to heed the warnings of God's prophets, the northern kingdom was overthrown by Assyria. Their years of sin, idolatry, injustice, greed, oppression, arrogance, hypocrisy, and immorality had finally led them to this. The Assyrians killed many of the people while others were taken into captivity. Israel ceased to exist as a nation and the people were taken from the land God had given them.

Judah existed as a nation for 136 years longer than Israel. This is probably because out of their ten kings, eight of them were good men who followed after God. Yet even with this advantage, the people of Judah still eventually fell into sin and turned away from God. Prophets like Jeremiah condemned Judah's apostasy, idolatry, moral decay, and perverted worship practices. They warned them that there would be serious consequences if they didn't turn back to God. Jeremiah was beaten, shunned, and imprisoned. Yet even in the face of such opposition, for forty years he continued to call God's people to repentance, but they never turned from their sinful ways.

When God saw that His chosen ones would not be deterred from their sin, He decided that enough was enough and judgment came to Judah through the Babylonians. Led by Nebuchadnezzar, the Babylonian army conquered Judah. Thousands of hostages were carried off to Babylon including Daniel and his friends. For the next seventy years the people of Judah suffered in exile, away from the land God had given them, because of their rebellion against God. Judah was never to exist on its own as an independent nation again.

> *The end is now upon you and I will unleash*
> *my anger against you. I will judge you*
> *according to your conduct and repay*
> *you for all your detestable practices.*
> Ezekiel 7:3

The decline and collapse of Israel and Judah came because God's people refused to follow God's ways and stubbornly did what was right in their own eyes. They followed after other false gods instead of the one true God. So they once again suffered the consequences of their sin.

Though they were unfaithful, God's faithfulness never ceased. Even while living in exile, the Lord used Daniel and Ezekiel to encourage His people to seek Him again. God had not deserted them but would preserve them and one day bring them back to their homeland. God was still going to fulfill His promise to bless the world through the descendants of Abraham, Isaac, and Jacob. He wasn't done with His chosen people yet.

"This is what the Sovereign LORD says: I will take the Israelites out of the nations where they have gone. I will gather them from all around and bring them back into their own land."
Ezekiel 37:21

Think It Over

God's love is everlasting. When we are faithless, He is faithful. When we are disobedient, He is patient. But like a wise parent, when we don't get it, God does what's best to help us grow up. Choices, limits, and consequences are an essential part of that process.

From the beginning God gave man choices. He wanted

people to choose to love Him with all their heart, soul, mind, and strength. Intentionally, by an act of their mind, will, and emotions. He wants us to love Him for who He is. To trust His ways and His words. To say no to what He says no to, and yes to what He says yes to. He wants us to willingly follow Him because we love Him and we recognize our need for Him.

In the Garden of Eden God told Adam and Eve they could eat fruit from a variety of trees that were there for them to enjoy. But He also set one tree apart from all the others. That one tree was off limits. When He said, "You are free to eat from any tree in the garden; but you must not eat from the tree of the knowledge of good and evil..." the Lord set a clear limit as a test of His children's faith, trust, and love for Him. The choice was theirs. The limit was clear. One tree.

Then God set out the consequences. "...in the day you eat of it, you will surely die." The incentive for choosing to obey God was high, in both what they had to gain and what they had to lose. It was a choice between life and death. Trust God, stay away from that tree, and have life. Do what you want instead of what God says, eat from that tree, and experience death. Tragically they chose to ignore God's limits. And because of that choice, life for them – and for all of mankind – has never been the same again.

For the nations of Israel and Judah the dreadful consequences were destined to come because of their bad choices. It was only a matter of time. But oh how different things could have been if they had done what the Ninevites did. If they had turned from their wicked ways and chosen to follow God's way instead of their own, they could have avoided years of pain and misery.

When God sets in place choices, limits, and consequences He does it for our own good. Like a loving parent, He wants us to learn to make the right choices. To learn from our mistakes and the mistakes of others. Like Israel and Judah, the Lord has set before each of us two choices: life in Him or death if we turn away from Him and go our own way. There will be very different consequences depending upon the choice we make.

Try Drawing It Yourself

Use the following simple sketch as an example and try drawing StoryBoard 9 to illustrate *Consequences*.

StoryBoard 10

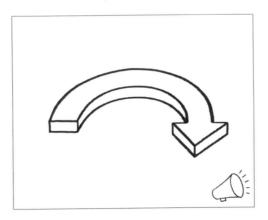

Return

After their time of exile, God was faithful to His word and brought His people back to their homeland in three phases over a period of 100 years. Though they came back to live in the land that was now ruled by others, they were home.

Once again God restored His children that they might enjoy a dynamic relationship with Him and be the people through whom the world would be blessed. And once again He called them to trust Him and follow His ways.

Return

BIG IDEA	God graciously brings His people home again.
Bible Books	Ezra, Nehemiah, Esther Haggai, Zechariah, Malachi
Main Cast	Zerubbabel, Ezra, Esther, Nehemiah
# of Years	100 years
Key Verse	*Jeremiah 29:14 - "I will be found by you," declares the Lord, "and will bring you back from captivity... to the place from which I carried you into exile."*

Dig Deeper Into the Storyline

Although God's people had turned their back on Him again and suffered the consequences in exile, He did not abandon them. As Jeremiah declared (see Jeremiah 29:10-14), the Lord faithfully brought His people back to their homeland. Hopefully their time spent in exile – suffering the consequences of their sin – had given them new incentive to faithfully walk with God and to set themselves apart from the evil ways of the nations around them.

Three prophets took center stage in God's plan to bring the people back to the promised land from exile. They came in three groups spread out over 100 years. The story of the first two returns is told in the book of Ezra and we read about the final return in Nehemiah. The book of Esther covers a period of time between the first and second returns when God providentially protected the Jews who were still living in Persia.

Fifty years after the Babylonian army destroyed the temple in Jerusalem and took the Israelites into exile, Persia overthrew Babylonia. Then Cyrus, the King of Persia, issued a decree that permitted God's people to return to their homeland. You'd think they would have immediately headed back home, but they didn't. After spending fifty years settling into their new lives in a new land, the thought of making a 900 mile trip back to the promised land wasn't that appealing. When **Zerubbabel** began organizing the group to return home, more than two million Jews chose to stay in Persia.

The faithful remnant made the long journey back to the promised land under Zerubbabel's leadership. Once they got home, he told them that their first priority was to restore worship of the one true God around the altar and to reinstate their religious feasts. This was accomplished during their first year back in the land. Their next priority was to rebuild the temple, so during their second year they laid its foundation, but then the work stopped due to opposition that discouraged and frightened them. So for the next eighteen years the temple sat unfinished while the people focused on building their own homes and their own lives. Things changed when God sent the prophets Haggai and Zechariah to encourage the people to put God's will and work first. With renewed commitment, the Children of

Israel got back to work on the temple and finally completed the task they had begun twenty years earlier.

During those years while the first group was returning to their homeland and rebuilding the temple and their homes, God still showed His love and faithfulness to the Jews who had chosen to remain in Persia. The story of **Esther** tells us how God providentially worked to protect His children from harm. A powerful Persian man named Haman, 2nd in rank to Persia's King Xerses, hated the Jews who had remained in Persia and came up with a plan to have all of them killed. But God had a plan of His own. He made it possible for Esther, a young Jewish girl with a heart for God, to become the Queen of Persia. From this position of influence with the King, Esther was used by God to save the Jews from death at the hands of Haman. Like a fairy tale ending, God's people lived while Haman was executed on the very gallows he had built to kill the Jews.

Fifteen years later, which was a little over eighty years after Zerubbabel led the first exiled group back to their homeland, **Ezra** was given permission by the King of Persia to take an offering to the rebuilt temple in Jerusalem. This opened the door for Ezra to lead a second group of Israelites back to their homeland. But Ezra was troubled once they got there. The people who had initially returned and rebuilt the temple had once again turned away from God. The priests and the people alike had married foreign women and followed their pagan ways. The horrible things Ezra saw the Israelites doing were appalling. Ashamed and embarrassed, Ezra wept and prayed and pleaded with God's people to confess their sins and turn from their evil ways and come back to God. The people were convicted by Ezra's words and a great revival came to Jerusalem as the people once again walked with God.

Over the years, reports about the progress in their homeland came back to those who were still in exile. When **Nehemiah** heard that the walls around Jerusalem were still in ruins and the city stood defenseless against enemy attacks, he was moved to tears and began praying that God would make it possible for him to lead another group of Jews back to rebuild the walls and fortify the city. God heard his prayers and sent Nehemiah back to the promised land with another group of Israelites. The task before Nehemiah proved difficult due to enemy opposition. But unlike Zerubbabel and the first group who wasted many years because of opposition and fear, with the help of God and the people's courage to persevere, the task of rebuilding the wall was completed in fifty-two days.

With many Israelites settling back into their homeland, the temple rebuilt, and a new wall around Jerusalem, the Children of Israel celebrated and recommitted themselves to God. They promised they would no longer marry foreign women and that they would follow God and obey His commands. Nehemiah then returned to Persia and reported back to the Jews who were still living there.

Unfortunately, before long God's children once again fell back into the evil practices of the pagan people around them. God intervened by sending the prophet Malachi to call them back to Him. He also sent Nehemiah back to Jerusalem a second time to call God's children to repentance. Even after all the years of Old Testament history to teach them about God and His power and love, the Children of Israel still struggled to love and live for God. But in spite of their weakness and sin, God continued to pursue them relentlessly. He remained faithful even when they were unfaithful.

Think It Over

God is God and we are not. While we give up on Him time and time again as we choose to live life in our own way, He never gives up on us. This was proven once again when God fulfilled His promise to gather His people from the foreign lands where they were in exile and bring them back to the homeland He had given them. He relentlessly continued to work out His plan to accomplish this massive effort over a period of 100 years.

God's love and grace and power are evident in so many ways during this time of returning to their land.

- He made it possible for Persia to become a leading world power that would eventually conquer the Babylonians and inherit the exiled people of Israel. Then amazingly the Persian nation treated the Jews favorably and allowed the people to each decide if they wanted to stay in Persia or return to their homeland.

Then the Lord raised up leaders with the calling, giftedness, and burden to do what needed to be done.

- Zerubbabel saw the importance of worship. He successfully led the people back to Jerusalem to begin worshiping God again through the practices and feasts that Moses had given them and to rebuild the temple.

- The prophets Haggai and Zechariah were each tasked with the responsibility of confronting the Children of Israel about their sin. They reminded them about who God was and who they were as His chosen people. They called them to be set apart from the evil ways of the world, and to return to God and a relationship with Him.

- Esther, a beautiful young Jewish girl, was placed in the King's palace "for such a time as this." In the right place, at the right time, her influence and courage saved God's people.

- Ezra was committed to helping God's people live right with the Lord and with each other. His life was devoted to studying the law of the Lord, and obeying it, and teaching the Children of Israel to do the same.

- Nehemiah was given the opportunity and responsibility to finish the work in Jerusalem so the city would be protected. The challenge was huge and dangerous, but God gave him the resources and perspective he needed, and what needed to be done got done.

With everything in place for things to finally run along smoothly in the people's relationship with God, you'd think everyone would have lived happily ever after. However, if you've been following these StoryBoards closely, you know the more likely outcome would be for the people to mess up again. And that's what they did.

- That's why God sent one more prophet. His name was Malachi and he was the last of the seventeen prophets that God sent throughout the times of the Kings, Consequences, and Return. He begged the people to turn from their wicked ways and to come back to God.

- And if that wasn't enough, God sent Nehemiah back to Jerusalem a second time, to once again remind the people of their previous commitment to be set apart from the sinful ways of the people around them and to walk closely with God and follow His ways.

What does all of that say to you?

God cares. God does not give up. God forgives. God is relentless in pursuing a relationship with us. God does whatever it takes to fulfill His promises to restore people. Sometimes He works in miraculous ways. Sometimes He works through normal people like you and me. Individuals who long to follow God's word and live in a loving relationship with Him and each other.

Try Drawing It Yourself

Use the following simple sketch as an example and try drawing StoryBoard 10 to illustrate *Return*.

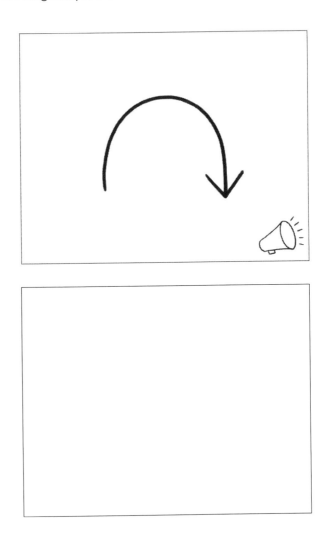

StoryBoard 11

Waiting

The historical period between the end of the Old Testament and the beginning of the New Testament is often called the 400 years of silence. During those years there were no prophets declaring God's word to the people. God was not showing up in clouds or burning bushes to get the people's attention. It was a time of silence from heaven. It was a time of waiting.

Though God was silent, He was still working. Final preparations were being set in place for the fulfillment of His promise to Abraham, Isaac, and Jacob to bless the world through their descendants.

During those 400 years, the world changed drastically. As Alexander the Great's empire spread throughout most of the known world, Greek became a common language. When the Roman Empire took over, roads were built and travel became much easier than it had ever been before. The things that happened in the world during these 400 years of silence paved the way for the coming of the promised Messiah.

Waiting

BIG IDEA	God quietly prepares the world for the coming of the Messiah.
Bible Book	None
Main Cast	Greece, Israel, Rome
# of Years	400 years
Key Verse	*Galatians 4:4a - But when the time arrived that was set by God the Father, God sent his Son...*

Dig Deeper Into the Storyline

Old Testament history ends around 425 B.C. with God's people back in the promised land after their time in exile. 400 years later, when we open the pages of the New Testament the southern area known as Judea, which included Jerusalem, is under Roman rule. This change was due to significant world events that occurred during those years between the closing events recorded in the Old Testament and the opening events that are recorded in the New Testament.

This gap of time is often referred to as the "400 silent years." Today as we look back at this time period it's evident that even though God was not speaking to His people through prophets or burning bushes, He was working through the political, spiritual, and social climate of the day to prepare the world for the Messiah, a descendant of Abraham, Isaac, and Jacob, that He had promised to send to bless the entire world.

During the first 100 years of this time, God's people enjoyed fairly peaceful conditions in their homeland under Persian rule. But dramatic changes followed when Alexander the Great established Greek rule throughout the known world. The Hellenistic culture was imposed on everyone and therefore became a way of life everywhere. Greek became the common language of the day, even for the Jews. The Old Testament scriptures were even translated into Greek during this time. This translation is known today as the Septuagint.

After Alexander the Great died at the age of 32, Judea came under the rule of Egypt and then Syria. Life under Syrian rule was a devastating time in Israel's history when the tyrannical King Antiochus Epiphanies forbid practicing any form of Judaism. Under the penalty of death, Jews were kept from observing the Sabbath or practicing circumcision or temple worship. Epiphanies disbanded the Jewish priesthood and set his own priests in their place. Unclean animals were sacrificed on the temple altar to Greek gods. The temple was dedicated to the pagan god Zeus. The Torah, the first five books of the law, was destroyed. The last straw came when Antiochus sacrificed a pig on the temple altar to Zeus on December 25, 168 B.C.

When that happened, the Jews decided they had had enough. When a Jewish man named Mattathias refused to worship the Greek gods, his act of courage in standing up to the Syrians and their evil ways began a rebellion. His son Judas Maccabees then rose up and led an army of Jewish rebels to victory. When faced with the daunting task of taking Jerusalem back from the Syrians, Judas' forces were outnumbered. His 10,000 troops were no match for the enemy army that numbered 65,000. Judas prayed for God's intervention and then led his forces to attack and set Jerusalem free. God gave them victory and they won back the city and reclaimed the Temple. On December 25, 165 B.C. the Temple was cleansed and rededicated with rejoicing and sacrifices for eight days. This monumental event is still celebrated by the Jews and is known as Hanukkah - the Festival of Lights. For the next 100 years the Children of Israel enjoyed a time of peace and freedom.

Judea eventually came under Roman rule when Pompey the Great attacked and conquered Jerusalem and slaughtered 12,000 Jews in 63 B.C. As the predominant world power during this time, the Roman Empire brought many changes throughout the land, including a new government, new laws, new leaders, new water and sewage systems, and roads that made travel throughout the entire Roman Empire possible. After that, all roads literally did lead to Rome. The Romans then remained in power and ruled over the Jews throughout the remaining silent years and also throughout the years that are recorded in the New Testament.

During the 400 years between the Old and New Testaments, God used the world powers of Greece and Rome to bring about major changes in the world that set the stage for the Messiah's coming.

- With Greek now a common language throughout the known world, the news about what God was going to do would be able to spread to all people.

- Dissatisfaction with religion was on the rise. Romans and Greeks alike were beginning to question the validity of polytheism and mythologies. Jews were struggling in their faith after being ruled over by godless foreign kingdoms and legalistic religious leaders of their own, and their longing for the promised Messiah grew.

- Since their return from exile, the Children of Israel had been in their homeland, but under the rule of foreign people. They achingly waited for God to once again send someone to deliver them from their oppressors.

- And along with all of this, when Rome came into power the world got smaller. The roads they built made it possible for God's message of love and forgiveness to spread throughout the world.

During these 400 silent years, the stage was set for God to fulfill His promise to bless the entire world through the descendants of Abraham, Isaac, and Jacob. The plan of redemption, that began so many years before when Adam and Eve chose to turn away from God, was about to be revealed – through the coming of the Messiah.

Think It Over

Times of silence don't mean that nothing is happening. What may seem like waiting too long, isn't, when God is working to set His perfect plan in place. If we could only see life from God's perspective, we would realize that He is always at work.

That was the case during the 400 years between the Old and New Testaments. When Old Testament history came to a close, the time was not yet right for the Messiah's coming. There was still more work to be done in the world before God fulfilled His promise. He used Alexander the Great and the spread of the Greek culture to set in place a common language that would make it possible for the message of God and His Messiah to be passed from person to person around the world. He let the Roman Empire build roads that would be used by the early Christians on their missionary journeys as they took their message to the world. Religious oppression led the people to long for a true loving relationship with God – something beyond what humans could accomplish on their own through legalistic religious practices. Could it be that God was working in these years to surface a need within the hearts of men once again for an intimate loving relationship with God?

400 years is a long time to wait for God to get in touch with man again. To let the Children of Israel know what was next in His plan to bring a lost world back into a relationship with Him. But important things were happening during those years as God prepared the world, and men's hearts, for the final phase of His plan – the fulfillment of His promise to Abraham and Isaac and Jacob – the coming of Jesus, the Messiah, to the world.

But when the time had fully come, God sent his Son, born of a woman, born under law.
Galatians 4:4

Not a minute too soon. Not a minute too late. But when the time was right. When the stage was completely set. When the final preparations were done. Jesus came.

In the world and in our lives, God does things right on time. But it's in His time. What to us may seem like waiting and waiting and waiting, is for a perfect reason. What may seem like silence, isn't. God is working.

Try Drawing It Yourself

Use the following simple sketch as an example and try drawing StoryBoard 11 to illustrate *Waiting*.

StoryBoard 12

Jesus

2000 years is a long time to wait for a promise to be fulfilled. Long enough to be forgotten. But God kept His promise when He sent Jesus—a descendant of Abraham, Isaac, and Jacob—into the world.

After the 400 years of silence, God spoke again – this time through His son. Jesus was the long awaited Messiah. The promised descendant of Abraham through whom the entire world would be blessed. In Him, God's plan for bringing man back into a loving relationship with Him was displayed for all to see. And this time the relationship wasn't dependent on man's obedience to God. This time it was based on God's work, not man's.

Jesus was born, grew up, ministered, died, rose from the dead, and went back to heaven – all within a short thirty-three years. Through all of that He fulfilled and revealed God's plan.

The historical account of Jesus' life is told in the first four books of the New Testament. Each is written by one of His followers. Each is unique in its approach, yet they are unified in their message. They finally reveal God's plan for saving man from his sin. For bringing man back into a relationship with God. Once and for all.

Matthew, Mark, Luke, and John tell us what God did to give us life now and forever, when He sent His own son to die for us, to pay the ultimate and final price for our sin. What He did was definitely worth the wait.

Jesus

BIG IDEA	God comes into the world as a man to bring man back to Himself.
Bible Books	Matthew, Mark, Luke, John
Main Cast	Jesus the Messiah
# of Years	33 years
Key Verse	*1 John 4:14b; 5:12 - The Father has sent his Son to be the Savior of the world. He who has the Son has life; he who does not have the Son of God does not have life.*

Dig Deeper Into the Storyline

We love good news. It beats the alternative. From "Johnny is finally potty trained" to "The doctor said I don't have cancer," we'll take good news any way we can get it. That's why the Gospels, the first four books of the New Testament, are a must read. And it's why some people read them again and again.

It's not that the historical time of the Gospels ushers in a new era where the problems man has been struggling with since the Garden of Eden are gone. It's that it's filled with good news that speaks right to our problems and gives us the solution. The Gospels give us the final answer to mankind's cycle of trying to walk with God and follow Him, only to fail and go our own way. Over and over again.

The Gospels – Matthew, Mark, Luke, and John – tell us the good news that's found in Jesus Christ. In fact, good news is the root meaning of the word Gospel. The Gospels masterfully tell His story. God's story. A story filled with hope in a problem-plagued world.

For 2,000 years God's people had clung to His promise to Abraham of a Messiah. A Savior. Someone who would save mankind from the awful consequences of the sinful nature that had infected every man, woman, and child. From Adam and Eve all the way up through the 400 years of silence and waiting, every attempt by mankind to live a sin-free life on their own had failed.

Man would try to follow God's ways and love Him and others as God had asked them to, but then they would fall back into sin and turn away from Him. Over and over again.

The simple fact is, if Adam and Eve couldn't do the right thing when they were living in a perfect world and literally walking with God day by day in the Garden of Eden, why would we ever think any of us could get things right in our own strength? We're just as frail and fallen as they were. And as we've seen time and time again throughout Old Testament history, sin brings death – physically, spiritually, and relationally – and it leaves mankind in a huge mess.

Jesus is God's promised answer. He did for us what we could not do for ourselves.

The four Gospels present an abundance of proof that Jesus is God's Son, the promised Messiah. He came into the world as a baby, born to a virgin. He grew up like you and me but without ever doing anything wrong (that would have been hard to take if you were one of his sinful siblings). And then at about thirty years of age Jesus announced that He was the Messiah and for the next three and a half years He did what His Father had been doing for the past 4,000 years since Adam and Eve fell into sin. He intentionally pursued sinful people like you and me so He could save us and bring us into a loving relationship with God and each other.

Jesus did everything needed to make it possible for us to have life now and forever. And unlike the people of the Old Testament who tried time and again to get it right in their own power, that life is now freely given to all who believe and embrace the good news that is declared in the Gospels.

- **Matthew** begins his account with a genealogy that traces Jesus' lineage back forty-two generations to show that He descended from Abraham. Writing primarily to a Jewish audience, this Jewish tax collector turned Christ-follower shows Jesus' Messianic credentials.

  Matthew goes to great lengths to help his Hebrew audience see that Jesus is the fulfillment of God's promises, by quoting or alluding to over a hundred Old Testament Scriptures as proof that Jesus is the Messiah, the true King of the Jews. From the prediction of His birth in Bethlehem (Micah 5:2/Matthew 2:1) to His death and His followers' abandonment (Zechariah 13:7/Matthew 26:31), to His resurrection (Psalm 16:10/1 Cor 15:3-8), Jesus' life backs up His claim to be the Son of God – the promised Messiah through whom the entire world would be blessed.

  The Gospel of Matthew tells us the good news that now, because of the work of Jesus on the cross, anyone who comes to believe that He is the Son of God who paid the price for our sins can have a relationship with God in His Kingdom forever.

- **Mark** focuses on Jesus' intentional life of sacrifice. Writing primarily to a Gentile audience and a culture that was well acquainted with slaves and sacrifices, Mark longs to see all people come to know and follow the One who became a servant to all and made the greatest sacrifice of all.

  The Son of God left heaven and came to earth and lived as an ordinary human. As a servant He healed the sick, fed the hungry, paid His taxes, ate with outcasts, challenged the religious, went without food in the wilderness, submitted to baptism, needed rest, wept with the hurting, restored the broken, uttered no threats when belittled and beaten, forgave undeserving offenders.

  And ultimately Jesus, as a servant, fully submitted His will to God's by dying on a cross to pay the price for our sins. Jesus told His followers that greatness in this life is found in servanthood. In living like He lived. In abandoning our will for God's will. And when we give up our life for Him, we gain everything. Serving is what a true follower of Christ does.

- **Luke** traces Jesus' lineage all the way back to Adam, which makes sense because Luke was a doctor and he was not a Jew. He was a very educated Greek man who became a believer and follower of Jesus. His Gospel account focuses on Jesus' humanity and complete dependence on God. He presents Jesus as both the Son of God and the son of man.

Jesus was born of a virgin and became a man so we could become children of God. And as His children we can become more and more like Jesus and our heavenly Father – living lives of love and good deeds. Not that our good deeds will ever make us perfect. They won't. The history of the children of Israel in the Old Testament proved that to us.

But God wants Jesus to live in and through us in the midst of this fallen world through the things we do, and what we think, and how we love and give and serve and speak. Following God's leading, and not our own way. Surrendering our will and our plans for His, so that in becoming more and more like Jesus we might become everything God designed us to be.

This "become all you can be" message had a direct connection to the Greek culture in Luke's day. Very much like people today, they were focused on reaching their fullest potential through education, the arts, sports, and occupations. With this audience in mind, Luke wrote a prescription for living life to the fullest.

His Gospel tells us it begins, is maintained, and ends with Jesus.

- **John** was one of the three disciples who were closest to Jesus. He wrote the fourth Gospel to help people everywhere know that Jesus is God's Son, the promised Messiah, and that they too could receive the gift of life that He made possible through His death and resurrection.

Jesus repeatedly claimed to be the source of life. He said, "I am the bread of life...I am the light of the world...I am the way, the truth, and the life...I am the resurrection and the life." Jesus went on to declare that He came from heaven so we could have life and have it abundantly (John 10:10). A full life now and a forever life later.

Bold claims for sure, but Jesus backed up His words by who He was and how He lived. Of the thirty-seven miracles found in the Gospels, John only focuses on seven. But each one is carefully selected to show Jesus' ability to give life to all who believe in Him and who turn to Him as the promised Savior.

The greatest proof that Jesus was who He claimed to be came when He rose from the dead. Above all else, that fact separates Jesus from every other religious leader who has ever lived. Jesus beat death and provided a way for us to live after we die. John tells us the good news that no matter who we are, no matter what we've done, Jesus came to give life to all who believe and receive Him as their Savior and Lord.

The good news of God's story is told in the first four books of the New Testament. After years of waiting for the Messiah to come so man could be set free from their endless cycle of sin, God came and lived among us. His name was and is Jesus. He was sent by God to bring sinners back into a personal relationship with Him. Not a list of rules to obey or sacrifices to make, but a relationship.

Why? Because God loves us and He really does want a relationship with us! Just as we've seen over and over throughout the history that is told in the Bible. And now when we by faith receive the gift of life found in Jesus Christ we are given this new life which changes everything, forever.

Think It Over

We're told there are about 130 million books in the world – give or take a few million. That's a lot of books. And that number continues to increase exponentially every year. That obviously means that no one, no matter how fast or ferocious his reading, will be able to keep up with every new book. Solomon got it right when he said:

*There's no end to the publishing of books,
and constant study wears you out so you're
no good for anything else.*
Ecclesiastes 12:12b

We agree! We only have so much time and so much energy. And when it comes to books, there will always be more to read and more to study and more to learn than we have time or energy for. But Solomon's point isn't that we should give up reading and studying and learning. Not at all. He is suggesting that we need to make the most of what we read within the limited amount of time and energy that we have.

Of the millions of books already in print, and the millions yet to be published, I want to encourage you to devote priority time and energy to the first four books of the New Testament – Matthew, Mark, Luke, and John. Why? Because they are words of life. What Jesus said and did can transform our souls. The words in these four accounts of Jesus' life not only show us the way to come into a loving relationship with God, but they can also liberate us from worry, self-centeredness, immorality, pride and arrogance, purposelessness in life, legalistic attitudes and perspectives, joyless living, empty religion, idolatry, selfishness, hatred, bitterness, pain, and fear. There is no end to the good that can come from reading what Jesus said and did.

Our world is filled with bad news. Evil and wickedness are everywhere. We hear it and see it all around us. Watch any newscast, any day of the week, and see for yourself that the majority of news is bad. Tragedy is everywhere. But 2,000 years ago good news came into this broken world. And it's news that can still change lives today. They are words that tell us about the fulfillment of God's promise to Abraham, Isaac, and Jacob to bless the world through their family. It's the truth that can set us free.

It's no wonder that when Jesus was born, when the long-awaited Messiah finally made His entrance into this fallen world, a host of angels told some lowly shepherds out on a hillside:

> *"Do not be afraid. I bring you good news*
> *of great joy that will be for all the people.*
> *Today in the town of David a Savior has*
> *been born to you; he is Christ the Lord."*

In a world that is desperate for good news, God keeps His promises and provides it. Jesus Christ is the way, the truth, and the life. He is our Savior. The one who makes it possible for us to have a permanent loving relationship with God – a relationship that is based on God's work and not ours. And He gives that life to all who believe and receive this gift.

Try Drawing It Yourself

Use the following simple sketch as an example and try drawing StoryBoard 12 to illustrate *Jesus.*

StoryBoard 13

Holy Spirit

During the time of Old Testament history God placed His Spirit, and His power, within specific individuals for specific purposes and times. But most of the time throughout those years, and through the 400 silent years and the thirty-three years that Jesus was living here on earth, the vast majority of people were on their own, trying in their own strength to obey God and walk with Him. And they failed over and over again. For thousands of years the ability to truly and completely walk with God seemed impossible.

God knew that mankind needed help. That's why He sent Jesus to live and die for us. His death on the cross paid the price for our sins, and made it possible for us to truly walk with God. But man was still living in a fallen world, surrounded by sin. And men were still living in the same bodies that were, by nature, prone to do things our own way instead of God's. Though their eternal future was secure because of Jesus, man still needed help.

Before Jesus left to go back to heaven He told His followers to wait in Jerusalem and God would send a helper. Someone who would make it possible for them to obey God and follow Him. Someone who would counsel them and lead them and fill them with power.

Ten days later God sent the Holy Spirit to live within all those who had chosen to believe in Jesus and follow Him. From then on, He would no longer live in a tent or building, or be placed in specific people for a short time for a specific purpose and then taken away again. Instead the Holy Spirit would live inside all those who accepted the gift of life through Jesus, permanently.

Throughout the following years Jesus' followers saw firsthand what can be done in and through God's people when they are filled with His Spirit. Thousands came to faith in Christ as the kingdom of God – the church – grew and spread throughout the world. And it continues to grow today.

Holy Spirit

BIG IDEA	God lives within those who believe in Jesus.
Bible Book	Acts
Main Cast	The Church, Jews, Samaritans, Gentiles
# of Years	30 years
Key Verse	Acts 1:8 - *"But you will receive power when the Holy Spirit comes on you; and you will be my witnesses in Jerusalem, and in all Judea and Samaria, and to the ends of the earth."*

Dig Deeper Into the Storyline

The story of Jesus' life and ministry continued through His followers. After His death and resurrection Jesus spent an additional forty days on earth preparing His disciples for His coming departure (Acts 1:3). His numerous appearances after His death and resurrection convinced His followers that He was the Messiah. What they saw and heard over those forty days changed them forever – and ended up changing the world. They went from fearful to fearless; from doubt to certainty; from devastated to rejoicing; from denying Jesus to unashamedly publicly proclaiming allegiance to Him.

This kind of transformational change needed to happen if they were to successfully carry out the worldwide mission Jesus had given them.

"Therefore go and make disciples of all nations, baptizing them in the name of the Father and of the Son and of the Holy Spirit, and teaching them to obey everything I have commanded you. And surely I am with you always, to the very end of the age."
Matthew 28:19-20

Before Jesus left His followers to go back to heaven, He gave them a job to do. They were to go to every nation in the world and tell them what Jesus had done for them through His life and death and resurrection. They were to let everyone know that it was possible for anyone, Jew or Gentile, to come into a relationship with God through the Messiah that had paid the price for their sins. Then all who embraced Jesus as their Savior were to be baptized and taught to obey all that Jesus had told them to do, which included going out and making more disciples.

The promise God had given so many years ago to Abraham had finally been fulfilled. The Messiah had come! The penalty for our sin had been paid. Jesus' work had made it possible for man to have a permanent relationship with God. And it was time for the disciples to let the world know this incredible news. God had prepared the world. Now He would prepare the followers of Jesus to take the message to the world.

The challenge before them was great. Actually, it was too big for them to handle. We've seen clearly throughout both Old and New Testament history that man's good intentions fall way too short. In our own strength, we fail. So before He left, Jesus promised to send the Holy Spirit who would give them the power to do all that He had commanded them (Acts 1:4-5). He would make it possible for them to get the job done.

So before they tried to do anything on their own, they were told to wait. 120 followers of Jesus gathered in a room in Jerusalem and prayed and waited (Acts 1:14-15). After ten days, just as Jesus said, the Holy Spirit miraculously came into them. From that point on, God no longer lived inside a building built by human hands, or temporarily in those God choses for a special task, but He now lives permanently inside His followers. And He gave them the power to do the work Jesus had set before them.

Acts is usually referred to as the Acts of the Apostles. This is understandable because the focus in Acts is on how the original Apostles, minus Judas and plus Paul, took the news about Jesus to the entire known world. But it's important to know that the amazing apostolic acts would not have been possible without the work of the Holy Spirit. The book of Acts focuses on the work of the Holy Spirit fifty-seven times. It tells us that the Holy Spirit fills, baptizes, empowers, saves, convicts, guides, reveals sin, commands action, inspires words, selects, communicates, works miracles, teaches, calls, sends, warns, qualifies, and predicts.

Throughout the historical time recorded in the book of Acts, we see the work of the Holy Spirit through Christ's followers as they carried out the mission Jesus had set before them. When Peter preached his first sermon (Acts 2:40-41) 3,000 people believed and turned from their sins to God because of the Holy Spirit's work in Peter and in the hearts of the people. And as others came to know and believe the news about Jesus, the Holy Spirit came into their lives too and also began working through each of them.

During this time those who chose to believe in Jesus and follow Him became known as Christians. Groups of these believers who gathered together regularly in homes were known as the church. They met to encourage each other to love and good deeds, to pray together, to eat together, to teach each other, to worship God together, and to help each other. They lived life together. As a local group of believers they tried to carry out Jesus' commission by showing God's love and grace in tangible ways to the lost world around them, always being ready to tell them the good news about what Jesus had done for them. And as the message spread throughout the world, the body of Christ grew by the work of the Holy Spirit in and through His followers.

Jesus was right. The mission He sent His followers to do could not have been done in their own strength. Without the Holy Spirit they could not have accomplished the great work that God had planned to do in the world. So God placed His Spirit inside those first 120 followers who were waiting for help, and then in all those who believed their message about Jesus, and on and on as each new believer trusted in Jesus as their savior. His plan was to work in and through His followers to spread the good news about what He had done for man through Jesus. And that is exactly what happened when the Holy Spirit came and worked in the lives of people. And the good news spread throughout Jerusalem (Acts 1-7), and then to Judea and Samaria (Acts 8-12), and then to the entire world (Acts 13-28).

Think It Over

It's amazing when you look at the people God entrusted with the task of telling the entire world about the incredible thing He had done to bring mankind back into a relationship with Him. These men and women, Jesus' frightened and confused followers, were just ordinary people. They each had strengths but they also had some significant weaknesses. Yet God chose to give them the responsibility to tell the world about what Jesus had done.

But He didn't leave them alone with that task. He knew on their own they would fail, just like men had been failing in their attempts to follow God since Adam & Eve. But because of Jesus' death on the cross, the Holy Spirit could now come and live permanently inside every person who believed. He would make it possible for His followers to fulfill the job Jesus had given them.

And after waiting for ten days, the Holy Spirit came upon those 120 people and they went out and changed the world.

The New Testament puts the spotlight on the importance of the Holy Spirit. We are to be filled with the Spirit (Eph 5:18); walk in the Spirit (Gal 5:16): not quench (1 Thes 5:19) or grieve (Eph 4:30) the Spirit: be led by the Spirit (Rom 8:14), live by the Spirit (Gal 5:25); and manifest the fruit of the Spirit (Gal 5:22-23) – love, joy, peace, patience, kindness, goodness, faithfulness, gentleness, self-control. When we are weak, the Holy Spirit fills in the gaps. God has given us everything we need, through the work of Jesus and the Holy Spirit within us, to walk with God and share His story and His love with the world.

The Apostle Paul on one occasion came across a group of people who were attempting to live the Christian life in their own strength by self-imposed rules and works. He wasn't impressed. He bluntly asked them, "*How foolish can you be? After starting your Christian lives in the Spirit, why are you now trying to become perfect by your own human effort?*" (Galatians 3:3 NLT) It's human nature to try to live life in our own strength. To try to do it ourselves. To be in charge. But when we do that, we either fail miserably or we end up missing out on the incredible work God could have done if we had let Him work through us.

Today, the good news about Jesus and what He did on

the cross for us has spread throughout the world. And it's because of those 120 frightened and confused followers of Jesus who, through the power of the Holy Spirit, stepped out in faith and spread the word. And it's continued to spread through His followers for 2,000 years, so that now we too can hear and believe the truth about what Jesus did for us. And as we accept God's gift of forgiveness and life through Jesus, the Holy Spirit also comes into us and works through us to spread the news and change the world.

Try Drawing It Yourself

Use the following simple sketch as an example and try drawing StoryBoard 13 to illustrate *Holy Spirit.*

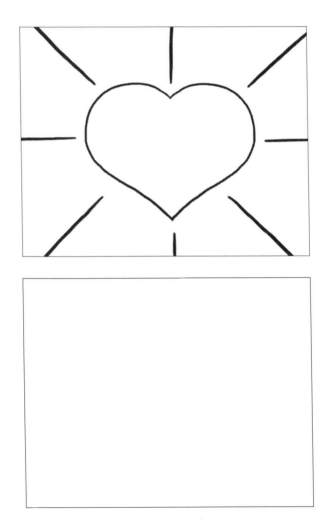

StoryBoard 14

Making Disciples

Before Jesus left to go back to heaven, He gave His followers specific instructions to go into the world and make disciples. So that's what they did. With the help of the Holy Spirit, they told everyone who would listen what God had done for them through Jesus and how they could now have an eternal relationship with Him. As more and more people came to believe, the early church was born and grew from city to city.

The apostles also had the responsibility to instruct the new disciples in all that Jesus had told them. They faithfully passed this information on as *the church* gathered, usually in homes, to learn, and to encourage each other, and to live life together. Five of the apostles also began writing letters that could be passed from home to home and city to city and eventually throughout the world. These twenty-one letters were filled with clear teaching about what God had done through Jesus, and also practical instruction on how a true disciple of Jesus should live.

Thousands of new believers became disciples of Jesus and began the adventure of living for Him and like Him. Their story – the teachings they heard and taught, the challenges they faced, the transformation they experienced, the amazing work they did – is found in the letters of the New Testament.

This particular StoryBoard – Making Disciples – is unique from all the others in a very awesome way. Though the letters of the New Testament were all written within a sixty-year span of time, the era of making disciples continues today. Almost 2,000 years later, we are still living in this time of history! The good news is still being passed from person to person. New disciples are still being made. God is still waiting for all those who will believe to come into a relationship with Him. And this era will continue until the day that God has planned for the final StoryBoard to begin.

Making Disciples

BIG IDEA	Helping people come to Christ and become like Christ.
Bible Book	Romans—Jude
Main Cast	The Apostles, Paul, Christ-followers
# of Years	60+ years then (2000+ years now)
Key Verse	*Matthew 28:19-20a - "Therefore go and make disciples of all nations, baptizing them in the name of the Father and of the Son and of the Holy Spirit, and teaching them to obey everything I have commanded you."*

Dig Deeper Into the Storyline

The twenty-two letters found in the New Testament give us a glimpse into the exhilarating and often challenging adventure that took place as Jesus' followers lived out His final instructions. He had told them to GO to the world and tell people what God had done for them through Jesus. They were to BAPTIZE those who believed. And then they were to TEACH them all that Jesus had taught them (Matthew 28:19-20) so these new believers could also live like Jesus and go out and make disciples. Jesus told them to start in Jerusalem and then take the message out into the rest of the world.

Peter and John, two of Jesus' original twelve disciples,

began this mission when Peter fearlessly stood up and called the Children of Israel who lived in Jerusalem to turn to Jesus for forgiveness of their sins and then tell others about their new faith by being baptized. In response to his words that day, 3,000 people believed and began to walk as followers of Christ.

As the good news continued to spread throughout Jerusalem, thousands more came to believe in the death and resurrection of Jesus. And as they came to believe, they were immediately baptized. The act of baptism symbolized how Jesus had washed their sins away and given them new life. Unashamedly and courageously, every new believer announced their faith and their love for Jesus by being baptized in front of their families, friends, strangers, and even enemies, as Jesus had commanded.

As the Gospel spread throughout Jerusalem, the city was changed as people were changed. Large groups of new disciples met publicly in the temple courtyard to pray and worship and proclaim the truth about the Messiah to whomever would listen. Small groups met in homes where they ate together, prayed, worshiped, studied the Old Testament Scriptures, talked about the life and teachings of Jesus, and encouraged each other to live lives characterized by love and good deeds. These new disciples, who came to be known as Christians, were being transformed as they lived life together. Just as Jesus had commanded, disciples were making disciples who were making disciples...

Sadly, many of the Children of Israel, including most of their religious leaders, refused to believe that Jesus was the Messiah they had been waiting for. And it wasn't long before they began persecuting anyone who became one of His followers. A man named Saul was one of the strongest opponents of Jesus' early disciples, even to the point of supporting the death penalty as Stephen became the first martyr for preaching the truth about Jesus.

Saul continued pursuing Christians wherever he went. Some lost their lives. Some were thrown in prison. Many were forced to flee Jerusalem and spread throughout the surrounding regions of Judea and Samaria. Which actually was right where God wanted them to be, since the second phase of His plan was to take the good news about Jesus out of Jerusalem and to the Jews who lived in Samaria and Judea. And that's what they did. Their mission to make disciples continued to grow and expand throughout the promised land.

As the number of disciples continued to grow and spread throughout the region, letters were written and passed from group to group, from church to church, to encourage the new believers and to keep them grounded in the truth and living like Christ. James, Jesus' brother, is thought to have written the first letter to those who had scattered after the persecution began in Jerusalem.

As Saul was relentlessly pursuing the early church in his attempt to stop the spreading of their message, he had a miraculous encounter with God. He ended up turning from his sin, accepting God's gift of forgiveness through Jesus, and becoming a follower of Christ. From that day on he turned all his energy and passion into spreading the truth about what God had done for man through Jesus Christ. God changed Saul's name to Paul and gave him a special assignment – to begin spreading the news about Jesus beyond the Children of Israel and into the rest of the world. Focused on the Gentiles, Paul ended up going on three missionary journeys to preach salvation in Christ throughout the known world including Asia, Greece, and Rome.

After traveling to cities like Colossae, Ephesus, Philippi, Thessalonica, Corinth, and Rome on his journeys, Paul then wrote thirteen letters (possibly fourteen if he authored Hebrews) to them after he left to encourage them and correct them. He challenged them to walk worthy of the life they now had through Christ and to continue to make disciples. Over a period of more than thirty years, Paul carried out Jesus' disciple-making mandate. He put the roads that the Romans had built during the 400 years of waiting to good use as, through the power of the Holy Spirit within him, he carried God's message of grace and forgiveness throughout the known world. Then after being imprisoned in Caesarea, a perilous ship ride to Rome, and two more imprisonments in Rome, Paul was put to death because of his faith in Christ.

Peter, Jude, and John are also among the five that wrote letters that were eventually passed around from city to city and ended up in the Bible that we have today.

- Like James, Peter wrote two letters to strengthen the faith of Christians who were scattered throughout Asia due to persecution. He encouraged them to endure their troubles as they focused on the living hope that was theirs in Christ.

- Jude's letter gave much needed counsel for standing against false doctrine and heretical teachers that were trying to lead God's children away from the truth.

- The Apostle John wrote four of the five final letters that we now find in the New Testament. Each continues the disciple-making focus by zeroing in on three main topics: how one can know for sure they are saved (1 John); how to respond to false teachers and their teaching (2 John); how to walk in the truth with each other (3 John). The book of Revelation, John's final letter, encourages believers in light of God's future plans to love the Lord with all their heart, soul, mind, and strength...to the very end.

Think It Over

It's not complicated. God asks us to love Him and to

love others. And if we're really doing that, we'll be making disciples. From the very beginning, that was God's plan – to bring people into an intimate loving relationship with Him and with each other. And that was also Jesus' plan. We see it in His life and in the instructions He gave to His disciples. And even to this day, almost 2,000 years later, His followers are to go and make disciples. This StoryBoard is where *we* come into the story of God. This era of history isn't finished yet. It continues on.

Those who truly love God and others will follow Jesus' instructions and *go*. Jesus adamantly stated how important it is that His disciples live in the world, without the world living in them. We are to be a tangible example of Christ among the lost people around us – in our homes, communities, work places, schools, and recreational pursuits. Going requires living among. Being like Jesus in what we say and do. Being the church and not just going to church. Showing our love for God and others through our actions and our words. Like the early disciples lived missional lives, we are to do the same.

Those who believe and become disciples of Jesus are also to be *baptized*. They are to publicly declare their belief in and commitment to Jesus. Baptism is meant to be an immediate first step after salvation, announcing to everyone that you have accepted God's forgiveness through Jesus and are now a follower of Christ. It's a command for new believers to obey and a sign for others to see and hear. Every disciple of Jesus should be baptized and should encourage other believers to do the same. Theologian FF Bruce got it right when he said, "The idea of an unbaptized Christian is simply not entertained in the New Testament."

But making disciples doesn't stop with baptism. New disciples are to follow the teachings of Jesus and show His love and grace to the world in tangible ways through their lives. That's why Jesus instructed His disciples to teach those who come to Christ *to do* all that Jesus commanded. It's not enough that we *know* what Jesus taught. What matters most is that we *do* what Jesus taught. In fact, the apostle John said the proof that one loves Jesus is that they do what Jesus commanded (John 14:15). He even went so far as to say, "*The man who says, 'I know him,' but does not do what he commands is a liar, and the truth is not in him*" (1 John 2:4). We cannot divorce *doing* from *knowing*. Jesus made that clear. The truth we say we believe must transform our lives. That's why God led James, Peter, Paul, John, and Jude to write the words found in the twenty-two New Testament letters. And what is it that Jesus commands us to do? It's the same thing that God has asked of man since the beginning of time as we know it. He wants us to love Him and to love others. That's it.

The bottom line – those who come to Jesus are to live like Jesus and they are to make disciples who make disciples.

Try Drawing It Yourself

Use the following simple sketch as an example and try drawing StoryBoard 14 to illustrate *Making Disciples.*

StoryBoard 15

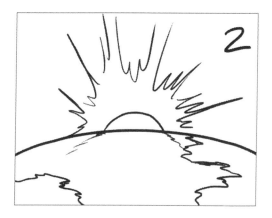

New Beginnings

Unique from all our other StoryBoards, this one is about an era that hasn't happened yet – a time in the history of mankind that is still to come. The book of Revelation, the last book in the Bible, is the record of God's planned re-creation. It's what lies ahead for all mankind.

Revelation tells how God will judge evil and eliminate it, once and for all. And it's about how He will create a new heaven and a new earth for all those who have received salvation through Jesus' work on the cross. This perfect world, inhabited by people who are walking in a perfect relationship with God and each other, will finally become a reality. God's long-awaited promise will be fulfilled. Through Jesus, a descendant of Abraham, Isaac, and Jacob, the entire world will be blessed.

New Beginnings

BIG IDEA	Life with God like it was meant to be...finally!
Bible Book	Revelation
Main Cast	God, Jesus, Satan, Angels, Believers
# of Years	Infinite Future
Key Verse	Revelation 1:19 - *"Write, therefore, what you have seen, what is now and what will take place later."*

Dig Deeper Into the Storyline

In Genesis, the first book of the Bible, we were told how life on earth began and how man chose to turn away from God. Then man continued to turn away over and over again throughout the history recorded in the rest of the Bible. The book of Revelation, a letter that became the last book of the Bible, reveals the new beginning that's promised for all those who accept God's gift of forgiveness through Jesus and choose to follow Him while they are walking through this fallen world. And the new beginning that's described will be better than anything that has come before.

John, who was the last survivor of the original twelve apostles, wrote the book of Revelation as a letter to seven churches who then passed it on to other early Christians. God led John to write about what was currently happening in his present time and also about what was yet to happen in the future (Revelation 1:19). Through John, God encouraged the believers of that day and also told the world how the story of His relentless pursuit of a relationship with man is going to end.

What was happening: John was in exile on a small Greek island called Patmos when God miraculously revealed His plan to him. Primarily focused on the future, what John wrote was a great comfort and encouragement to the early Christians who were being persecuted mercilessly at that time by Nero. And that blessing and encouragement can also be ours when we hope in Jesus, the one who is at the center of attention in Revelation. He is the one "*who is, who was, and who is to come*" (Revelation 1:8).

John was ninety years old when he wrote this letter. During the sixty years he had lived since Jesus' death and resurrection, he had seen the good news spread "to the uttermost parts of the world," just as Jesus had commanded. Thousands, if not millions, of people had come to believe in what Jesus had done for them on the cross and had become His disciples. God's *church* was growing. Believers were meeting in homes throughout the known world. They were living life together and meeting in both large and small groups for encouragement, worship, prayer, instruction, and fellowship. When anyone had a need they sacrificially gave to meet those needs.

But the mission of the early Christians that started off so well gradually began to lose its impact as the years went by. For some, the excitement and passion of their young faith in Christ began fading. The love these early believers had for the Lord began to get lost in the cares of their day-to-day lives. Revelation 2 & 3 is a record of the spiritual lethargy that was infecting the church by the time John wrote this letter.

Their first love – their love for God – had been replaced with the love of lesser things. Fear had overwhelmed faith. False teaching had distorted the truth. Immorality was being tolerated. Though they were still called Christians (which literally means *little Christs*) many of them were no longer living like Christ or for Christ. Instead of being on fire for God, they were lukewarm or cold when it came to following Jesus' example in their day-to-day lives.

God wasn't happy. He instructed John to remind them of the life and mission He had given them. To encourage them to count the cost and turn back to God. How they responded to His words to them through John would impact what would come next, for them personally and for the world. Jesus was standing at the door knocking. Waiting. Would they turn from their self-centered ways and come back to the Lord? He was ready and eager to share an intimate relationship with them. But is that what they wanted? Once again, the choice was theirs.

What was going to happen: After challenging the early

Christians to get their act together, John then gave them a powerful glimpse into God's future plans. John was filled with both fear and awe at the vision God gave him of what was to come. It was both devastatingly horrible and amazingly hope-filled. For good or bad, once and for all the ultimate consequences of man's choices would be realized.

What God revealed to John about the future has led to many debates over the years about what it all literally means. The images he describes are very colorful and bold, and make it hard for us to pin down the specific events that will happen. But the bottom line of what will happen is very clear. Jesus will return and set things right, once and for all.

John's look into the future included seeing twenty-one different judgments (Revelation 4-18) that will one day come upon this fallen world. Described as seven seals, seven trumpets, and seven bowls, each of these judgments graphically showed the utter devastation that is yet to come to planet earth.

Just as the Old Testament predicted a "time of Jacob's trouble," John saw a seven-year period of time that is coming when all hell will literally break loose and bring cataclysmic destruction to earth. Disaster and tragedy will fill the world due to war, economic meltdowns, plagues, disease, rampant killing, massive earthquakes, hail, fire, the death of life in the sea, the destruction of ships, falling stars, poisoned and bloody drinking water, the sun and moon darkened, supernatural darkness everywhere, the heat from the sun overwhelming the earth and people, famine, governments falling, and satanic forces stealing away life and peace throughout the world. Millions upon millions of people will die and those who survive will want to die.

> *During those days men will seek death,*
> *but will not find it; they will long to die,*
> *but death will elude them.*
> Revelation 9:6

While life on earth during the beginning of the seven years will be terrible, it will get even worse. During the final three and a half years, a time of even greater tribulation will come as it leads up to the final battle of Armageddon (Revelation 16:16). On that day the forces of evil will wage war against God, but they will fail and will be completely destroyed. God will prevail as the armies of Satan are defeated.

After this great battle, Satan and his demons will be bound and locked into a dark abyss for a thousand years. For the first time in all of human history, the world will be free from their influence. With Satan, sin, and evil removed from earth for that time, Jesus Himself will rule on earth over those who survived the time of tribulation and those who had previously chosen to follow God and received new life through Him. Yet even during these years many of the survivors and their descendants will choose to go their own way instead of God's.

When the thousand years are over, Satan will be released from his prison and given one final opportunity to deceive people into turning away from God and following him, just as he did in the Garden of Eden with Adam and Eve. And sadly, many will choose to follow him. Then there will be one final battle and God will permanently cast Satan and all who chose to follow him into the Lake of Fire, which is also known as Hell. And they will remain there for eternity.

Though the image of seals and trumpets and bowls bringing judgments on the world is hard for us to grasp, the bottom line truth is clear. The fallen world will be punished for its wickedness, along with those who have turned against God and His ways. Those who have trusted in God and the life He offers through Jesus will be saved and set free from the pain and hardship of living in a fallen world. While evil will be justly punished, those who choose God will move on to the perfect future that God had desired from the very beginning.

After John was shown the devastating judgment that will come, he was given a look at the future we all long for – the new life and perfect world that will come to all who are saved through Jesus Christ (Revelation 19-22). Everyone who said yes to God's offer of a personal relationship with Him will be given a brand new life and a brand new place to live. At the end of the millennium, once Satan is sent to Hell for good, God will re-create a new heaven and a new earth for His followers to live in. A whole new world that He can enjoy with mankind as they live life together in loving relationship with Him and each other, just as He planned in the beginning. He will give us all a new beginning.

Jerusalem will be replaced with a New Jerusalem. It will be beautiful beyond belief and God will live there among His people forever. There will be no more sin. No more tears. No more pain or death. No more need for emergency rooms, hospitals, doctors, or morticians. No more drugs of any kind. No crime. No war, or guns, or bloodshed, or sweat. God will finally live among His people again and life will be like it should have been all along.

Think It Over

The Bible ends where it begins, with a choice. From the very beginning God intentionally chose to give man a choice. It's up to each of us to decide if we're going to do life His way or our own way. And as we've seen throughout the Bible and now in the book of Revelation, that choice is literally a matter of life or death.

The incredible glimpse of the future that God gave John tells of tragedy and triumph. For those who choose to turn away from God and go their own way, the end will be devastating. What God said from the beginning will come true. They will surely die. Having ignored God's invitation, commands, patience, grace, and relentless pursuit of a relationship with them, they will get what they wanted – life without God, forever.

Through chapter after chapter John paints the picture of how terrible life will be for those who reject God. Just the thought of worldwide disaster, disease, and death should be more than enough to convince anyone to choose the path to life. If you are still trying to decide which path you are going to take when it comes to God and what He's done for you through Jesus, the book of Revelation is His final attempt to convince you to choose life. Now. Before it's too late. The book is like a series of road signs warning you of upcoming disaster. Stop! Wrong way! End of road! Bridge out! It's up to you to decide whether or not you believe the signs Revelation posts.

God's not going to force anyone to join Him in heaven. He's leaving the choice up to you. But one day in the future, there will be a new heaven and a new earth where God and those who chose to follow Him will live together, forever. It will be a place for all who by faith said yes to a relationship with God through Jesus. It's for anyone who turns from doing life their own way to God's way. Those who accepted the gift God offered when He sent Jesus into the world to die on the cross for our sins, so it would finally be possible for us to have a relationship with Him again.

So the choice is yours. Our Bible StoryBoards end with the final showdown between good and evil. Good will win and live happily ever after. But how *your* story ends will depend on what you decide about God and Jesus. This life is filled with choices, but none is more important than this one. All who choose to come to God through Jesus for life will receive life. Now and forever. These are the ones who will be eagerly looking forward to Christ's return, when He will set everything right. He invites you to come.

> *The Spirit and the bride say, "Come!" And let*
> *him who hears say, "Come!" Whoever is thirsty,*
> *let him come; and whoever wishes, let him*
> *take the free gift of the water of life.*
> Revelation 22:17

Try Drawing It Yourself

Use the following simple sketch as an example and try drawing StoryBoard 15 to illustrate *New Beginnings.*

StoryBoard 16

Your Story

Bible StoryBoards has two primary purposes. One is to help you understand the simple yet life-changing story of the Bible. The second is to give you a tool so you can then share that story with others.

If you are a follower of Christ, when you use these StoryBoards to share with others – whether it's on your iPad or smart phone or a napkin – this is the point in the story that is yours. You too have a story. It's unique and personal to you. Now could be the perfect time to tell them about your relationship with the God that pursued you with His unending love.

If you haven't figured out yet how you fit into God's story, now is a good time to stop and consider what you will do with what you now know. Will you accept His love and forgiveness through Jesus? Will you choose to love Him in return? Will you enter into a new and everlasting relationship with God? It's available to all who will simply believe and receive this incredible gift.

CONCLUSION

No matter how much we may love someone, we can't make them love us in return. We can do our best to show them our love, but it isn't actually a love *relationship* unless they choose to love us too.

Just yesterday the matter of reciprocal love was at the heart of a conversation I had with a 24-year-old Ukrainian woman who thinks she's found the guy of her dreams. She loves him but she isn't sure yet if he loves her. So she's waiting, and hoping, and even praying that he'll come to love her like she already loves him.

The story of God that is told in the Bible is that kind of love story. It shows us that God loves us more than we will ever understand – deeply, genuinely, sacrificially. He knows everything about us and yet He still loves us and longs for us to love Him. And He has relentlessly pursued us in the hope that we will choose to walk in a loving relationship with Him.

Since man was first created, God has done everything possible to show us that love. And the Bible tells us the story of His relentless pursuit of us. We've seen it demonstrated over and over again throughout the ages. We've seen it brought to life in Jesus. And we see it in the greatest demonstration of love humanity has ever seen – Jesus' death on the cross for us.

And now God waits, like the Ukrainian woman I talked

to yesterday is waiting to see how her love story will play out. God waits to see what each of us will do. Will we choose to love Him and enter into a relationship with Him? Or will we turn our backs and walk our own way, as so many did over and over again throughout history?

What happens next is up to you.

If you have never had a personal relationship with God before, that's the decision you need to make now. Will you accept His love and forgiveness through Jesus? Will you choose to love Him in return? Will you enter into a new and everlasting relationship with God? It's available to all who will simply believe and receive this incredible gift.

If you've already taken the step of saying yes to a relationship with God through Jesus, your future has been changed for good forever. But don't forget that relationship with God begins now. He wants you to walk with Him day by day, growing in your love for Him and also in your love for others. And the best way to do that is to spend time talking to Him, and listening to Him, and reading His love story as revealed in the Bible. Allow His words to teach and guide you – to transform you. Let the liberating truths of Scripture go down deep into your soul and change you from the inside out.

And finally, now that you know God's love story, you can share it with others. As a follower of Jesus, you too have been given the responsibility of spreading the good news and making disciples. We want to challenge you to use these fifteen simple pictures to help others understand the story of God that is found in the Bible. Whether you do that by using our Bible StoryBoards app on your phone or iPad, or by sketching 15 simple pictures on a restaurant napkin as you talk through the story with a friend, be prepared to share the incredible story of God's love for us with others when you have the opportunity.

Whatever you do now, please don't ignore God's plea for a relationship with you. In Bible StoryBoards you've seen the disastrous consequences when we turn our backs on God. Don't let that happen to you. Make your relationship with God a priority. It will take intentional effort and sacrifice, but the reward is definitely worth it.

May you truly understand and accept the incredible love God has for you. And may you walk closely with Him, both in this world and forever.

Additional Resources

The StoryBoards Explained

The 15 Detailed StoryBoards

The 15 Simple StoryBoards

The Authors & Artist of Bible StoryBoards

StoryBoard 1

Beginnings

A picture of earth reminds us that God created the world and everyone and everything in it.

StoryBoard 2

Sin

Sin entered the world when Adam & Eve ate a piece of fruit from the one forbidden tree in the Garden of Eden. The Bible doesn't say what kind of fruit it was, so we draw an apple to represent whatever that fruit was.

StoryBoard 3

Chosen People

A family tree is used to represent the family God chose to work through to eventually bless the entire world. The four people on the tree are Abraham, Isaac, Jacob, and Joseph.

StoryBoard 4

Moses

This picture shows God, through Moses, parting the Red Sea.

StoryBoard 5

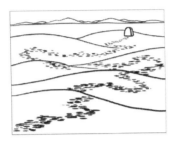

Wandering

A line randomly wanders around the page until it ends at a headstone which represents the death of the unbelieving generation.

StoryBoard 6

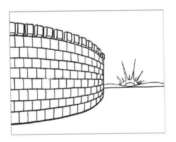

Promised Land

The walls of Jericho mark the first town the Children of Israel conquered as they reclaimed the promised land.

StoryBoard 7

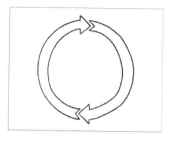

Judges

Two arrows create a never-ending circle representing the Children of Israel turning to God and then away from God, over and over again.

StoryBoard 8

Kings

The crown represents the Kings the people asked God to give them. The megaphone reminds us that during this time God sent prophets to warn the people and call them back to Him.

StoryBoard 9

Consequences

A sad face with tears is used to represent the tragic consequences of sin. The megaphone shows that the prophets continued to plead with the people to turn back to God.

StoryBoard 10

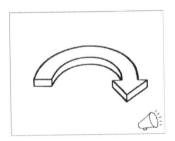

Return

A U-turn arrow shows that God brought His people out of exile and back to their land. And again the prophets spoke, which is represented by the megaphone.

StoryBoard 11

Waiting

The 400 silent years of waiting between the end of the Old Testament and the beginning of the New Testament.

StoryBoard 12

Jesus

Four books represent the first four books of the New Testament – Matthew, Mark, Luke, and John. The cross on the cover reminds us that these are the books that tell us about the life and death and resurrection of Jesus.

StoryBoard 13

Holy Spirit

Since Jesus' death and resurrection, the Holy Spirit now comes to live inside all who believe. We say that He is living in our hearts. The lines represent His power that now works in and through us.

StoryBoard 14

Making Disciples

We are to tell others about Jesus and help them become His disciples. Then they are to tell others about Jesus and help them become His disciples.

StoryBoard 15

New Beginnings

Here we draw another picture of earth, but with a two. This represents the new earth and heaven that God will create in the future when Jesus comes again.

The 15 Detailed StoryBoards

The 15 Simple StoryBoards

The Authors of Bible StoryBoards

Dave is a pastor who has degrees from Westmont College (Sociology), Talbot Theological Seminary (M Div), and Western Seminary (D Min). Over the years he has been the Lead Pastor at three churches and has taught several hundred Live Events for Walk Thru the Bible Ministries.

Bernice has a degree in Psychology and has focused on raising her family and leading various ministries in the church, particularly helping Music Pastors plan and lead worship services where people can connect with God and each other.

Today Dave and Bernice live in the San Francisco Bay Area where Dave is the Lead Pastor at Bridges Community Church in Los Altos. They are committed to helping people grow in their understanding of who God is and what it means to follow Him — which includes encouraging and equipping people to make disciples.

Along the way Dave has also hosted a weekday radio program and written four previous books—*Owner's Guide to Using Your Bible*, *Before You Live Together*, *Before You Get Engaged, and Just One More Thing: Before You Leave Home.* He'd tell you he couldn't have done any of that without Bernice by his side.

About the Artist

Andy Bates is a freelance artist from the San Francisco Bay Area. He has illustrated two children's books, including *How to Handle a Hippo*, and has also provided artwork and logo designs for several companies. During the day, he works as a software engineer in the Silicon Valley tech industry. When he's not working or drawing, he enjoys spending time with his wife Marcy, and his kids Trevor and Molly.

Additional resources, including the app version of this book, can be found at BibleStoryBoards.com

For more information about the Gudgels and their other books, visit their website at davidandbernice.com

Made in the USA
Charleston, SC
04 January 2015